Assembly Required

A CONTINUOUS SCHOOL IMPROVEMENT SYSTEM

LAWRENCE W. LEZOTTE ★ KATHLEEN M. MCKEE

Published by:

Effective Schools Products, Ltd.
2199 Jolly Road, Suite 160
Okemos, Michigan 48864
(517) 349-8841 • FAX: (517) 349-8852
http://www.effectiveschools.com

Assembly Required:
A Continuous School Improvement System
Call for quantity discounts.

Cover design by Erin Morrison
Book design by Brandy Church

Manufactured and printed in the United States of America.

ISBN 1-883247-20-9

Table of Contents

Assembly Required:
A Continuous School Improvement System

List of Figures

Assembly Required:
A Continuous School Improvement System

Introduction

Assembly Required:
A Continuous School Improvement System

Some Assembly Required. These words have struck fear into the hearts of many a brave soul as they faced the task of putting together a slew of unfamiliar parts into a workable form. Perhaps you, too, have experienced this fear as you assembled a bicycle, a swing set, or a new computer desk. If you're like most of us, you pushed on despite your trepidation, to complete your mission. Again, if you are like most of us, sometime during the process you encountered one or more obstacles. Perhaps you simply didn't have an accurate picture of what it should look like when it's done. Perhaps there were parts missing (which, of course, you didn't figure out until halfway through the process!). Maybe the directions just didn't make sense or were too complicated to follow. Or maybe you didn't have the right tools (you needed a flat-headed screwdriver and all you could find were two Phillips-head screwdrivers and a hammer, which at this point you were tempted to use).

Implementing school improvement—building an effective school—is much like assembling that swing set or desk. First, you must have an accurate picture of what an effective school looks like. Then you must have all the components and the right tools to build an effective school. Finally, you need clear, logical directions on how to use the tools to assemble all the components of an effective school in a way that best serves your students.

This publication is designed to give you the information, tools, and directions you need to become an effective school or district. We will use our swing set/desk analogy to frame the process. But remember, while our swing set/desk analogy is demonstrative, it lacks in one critical area. When you are finished assembling your swing set or desk, you're done. There is little or no maintenance after the item is put together. Continuous school improvement, on the other hand, is just that . . . continuous. It is a never-ending cycle of self-examination and adjustment. The effective school and district will continually ask *How are we doing? What can we do better? How can we better serve our students?* and make frequent adjustments in pursuit of the "learning for all" mission.

Part I of this book will provide you with an accurate picture of what an effective school looks like and an overview of the critical theories that provide the foundation for continuous and sustainable school improvement. You will learn how the key concepts and principles of Effective Schools research, Systems Theory, and Continuous Improvement are woven into one system of school change. This section will also outline the critical components of continuous school improvement, including an effective team, as well as describe and demonstrate the tools you will need to implement the concepts and principles into a successful, self-renewing school improvement implementation strategy.

Part II will then give you the "directions" on how the concepts, principles, and tools can be applied so that you can implement and manage continuous school improvement in your school or district.

Our promise to the readers is that, if a school or school district thoroughly and thoughtfully implements the recommended steps and strategies set forth in this manuscript, three things will occur. First, each school and the system as a whole will move toward excellence. Second, the improvements will be sustainable over the long term. Third, and most important, students will achieve at higher levels than ever before.

— Lawrence W. Lezotte

Part One

CONTINUOUS SCHOOL IMPROVEMENT
AND THE EFFECTIVE SCHOOL: THE BASICS

Part I

Continuous School Improvement and the Effective School: The Basics

There's an old saying, "If it looks like a duck, walks like a duck, and quacks like a duck, it must be a duck." But, if you don't know what a duck looks like, walks like, or sounds like, you still won't be able to recognize it. The same goes for continuous school improvement and the effective school. In order to implement sustainable school reform, you must become acquainted with the fundamental concepts of continuous school improvement.

The goal of this section is to give you an accurate picture of what your "swing set"—a.k.a. the effective school, sustainable school reform, and continuous school improvement—looks like.

Chapter 1

Essential Attributes and Critical Components of Sustainable School Reform

Essential Attributes

School reform is at or near the top of the current social/political agenda. When we examine what society wants in the name of reform and what research suggests is required to achieve those reforms, several essential attributes come into focus. Each of these attributes, to varying degrees, requires today's schools to approach reform differently than they have in the past. An effective model of school reform must encompass these attributes.

Focuses on Results

For most of the last century, schools were evaluated in accordance with the standards and processes set by the various regional accrediting bodies. While there were some regional differences in the accreditation standards and processes, they were more alike than different. Most of the regional accreditation standards examined inputs such as the number of fully certified teachers, how many books were in the school library, and the number of square feet of science laboratory space. Rarely, if ever, were schools specifically asked about student learning. Beginning in the 1980's, however, the "rules of the game" changed.

Many of the state education departments, propelled by political discontent, began to supercede the regional accreditation associations with their own evaluation models; thus, the era of output accountability was born. The accreditation process became more of a peer review evaluation process that relied heavily on a visiting team. Even more dramatically, the state accountability models sharply changed the focus to measured student achievement as the primary basis for judging schools.

While there is and always will be impassioned debate on how student achievement ought to be assessed, there is little doubt that the central standard for school evaluation will be student achievement—**results!** In the current school reform context, *any model of school improvement that is going to be useful to schools must focus explicitly on results, evidence of student learning, and student achievement.*

Simultaneously Considers Quality and Equity

Once the educational establishment accepts the fact that, right or wrong, the school and its teachers are going to be judged by student results, the question is then raised as to how student results should be examined. In the United States, with its deep—and hopefully unwavering—commitment to the democratic ideal of equality, schools will be judged on two standards. The first standard will be overall level of student achievement. The second standard will be equity, which will be evaluated by looking at the distribution of measured student achievement across various categories of students (boys compared to girls, minority students to nonminority, middle-class students to disadvantaged students). These indicators of quality and equity will be monitored over time because trend data is central to the notion of school reform.

Obviously, enduring models of school reform must incorporate tools and strategies that assist staff and administrators with documentation of the quality and equity dimensions of achievement within the school.

Data-Driven

Examining the level and distribution of student achievement data as measured by the state is perhaps the clearest example of what it means to be data-driven. In the context of school reform, however, this is but one type of data that schools must monitor, analyze, and report. To successfully reform themselves, schools must go much "wider" and much "deeper" with systems of data. For example, it doesn't do the school reformer much good to simply know the student's final scores on the state accountability tests. To improve student, and ultimately, school performance, teachers must know

specifically what curricular objectives the student did or did not master. Furthermore, waiting to get such in-depth information until after the accountability test is scored and returned is too late to do any good. Schools must develop data-driven systems for monitoring student learning that are much more *specific* and *frequent* if they are going to succeed on the mission of "learning for all."

Pertinent and timely data also helps focus our reform efforts on the real problem. For example, increasing time on a task may help students learn that task, as long as they are in school. However, increasing time on task for students who are often absent and for extended periods of time will do little to help. Unless the attendance problem is specifically solved, successful learning for these students will continue to elude the school.

Models of school reform that truly add value for the school on its continuous improvement journey must address the issue of being data-driven.

Research-Based

Any profession committed to improving itself must define and justify its activities and systems on the basis of research and documented proven practice. For over thirty years, education researchers have examined and evaluated schools and their practices to identify what works in educating children. As a result, we now have a huge body of research upon which to draw as we approach school improvement. Unfortunately, this knowledge base is often ignored or quickly dismissed when educators plan and implement instructional programs and strategies. Any effective model of school reform must be grounded in the research.

Collaborative in Form

School improvement, because it affects so many groups and individuals, cannot be done in a vacuum. Furthermore, any society committed to democracy must model the democratic process in those institutions charged with the task of educating its children. Future chapters of this book will show you how to make the process of continuous school improvement inclusive and collaborative.

Ongoing and Self-Renewing

School improvement is a never-ending process. The process is a cycle of action, evaluation, and reflection that should result in a continuous adjustment of our activities in response to a changing environment, new research on proven practices, and the success or failure of our previous efforts. The effective school reform model will incorporate this cycle of self-renewal.

The Continuous School Improvement Model presented within these pages addresses each of these issues. The processes and the tools associated with this model of school improvement will help you create and monitor a collaborative and inclusive system that is sensitive to both quality and equity, is grounded in the research, and is data-driven and self-renewing.

KEY CONCEPTS

An effective model of sustainable school improvement is:

- Results-Oriented

- Focused on both Quality and Equity

- Data-Driven

- Research-Based

- Collaborative

- Ongoing and Self-Renewing

The Continuous School Improvement Model is:

Critical Components: The Five T's

What are the essential components of sustainable school reform? School reform always begins in the head and heart of everyone who is willing to consider the topic. In that sense, each thinking individual begins the reform conversation with a "mental model" of the reformed school. If we examine an individual's mental model of school reform, we discover that it is composed of two dimensions: a vision of the reformed school, and a vision of how the school should set about achieving reform.

In this section, I offer my vision of the essential elements of sustainable school reform. They include the *Five T's*: theories, teams, time, technology, and tools. In subsequent sections, the elements are woven together to form the tapestry of continuous and sustainable school reform.

Theories

In its simplest form, a mental model or vision represents one's theory of how the world is or ought to be. In the context of sustainable school reform, a theory represents one's belief of what schools should do and be, and how a school should seek to achieve that vision. For example, a popular theory of school reform states that student learning will not improve unless schools implement a strict discipline code.

A major challenge facing school reformers is the lack of consensus among the various stakeholders as to the theories that should guide reform. The lack of consensus is apparent on both what school reform should look like and how best to achieve the goals of school reform. The model of continuous and sustainable school reform offered within these pages is based upon three powerful and time-tested theories:

The Effective Schools Model will provide a framework for designing and evaluating the effective school based on school improvement research. This body of research represents a theory or mental model of a school where the vast majority of its students can demonstrate mastery of the intended curriculum. Furthermore, the mental model of the Effective School states that effectiveness is the output of the interaction of several, alterable, school-level variables. If these alterable organizational and instructional variables are present and strong in a school, improved student learning will follow.

Systems Theory will help you recognize the interrelationships between every person, department, and process in your school and their various impacts on the change process.

Systems Theory states that a system is a network of interdependent components that work together to accomplish the aim of the system. Examination of this basic definition reveals three core beliefs that are extremely valuable in the context of sustainable school reform. First, existing schools represent a system-in-place. Second, the system-in-place is ideally suited to producing the results the school *is currently getting*. Third, any change in the desired results from the current system-in-place is going to require a change in the mission, core beliefs, and core values that underpin the system, especially if the goal is to permanently sustain the desired change.

Systems thinking does not occur easily for most educators and this re-orientation is itself a difficult reform for many teachers and administrators. This is due, in great part, to teacher education, as well as administrator training, which has emphasized the *psychology* of teaching and learning, and has not devoted much time or attention to the *sociology* of teaching, learning, and schooling.

Systems theory also serves to forewarn school reformers that change in a complex system like a school is neither simple nor easy. Those who have made a career of studying school change have been quick to discover how hard it is to install real change in a school and have it be sustained over time.

Continuous Improvement Theory. One of the fundamental beliefs that define continuous improvement is that excellence is always a goal and never a destination. It is, in fact, an endless journey. The notion that school reform is an ongoing, never-ending process runs counter to the ideas of many educators. Many believe that once we get the system set it can be maintained, without change, from then on.

Another core value of continuous improvement is the need for constant feedback from systems designed to monitor the current situation and adjust future actions. In the context of sustainable school reform, most schools do not collect and monitor the kinds of information that would be most useful in advancing the learning mission of the school.

Each of the three theories represents a complex area of study. Needless to say, they will not be treated with the breadth and depth that they deserve in this manuscript. Selected concepts and principles from each will be woven together to help schools achieve the goal of continuous and sustainable school reform. When taken together, these three models form a powerful technology for creating and sustaining positive change in schools, classrooms, and whole school districts.

Teams

Like most systems, schools are complex. They are made up of many pieces and parts and are maintained by many individuals. But because most teachers work alone in their respective classrooms with their own students, they don't see the interdependence that exists. They sometimes forget that one person's actions affect everyone else in the system to some degree.

Teamwork is a critical attribute to successful change in a complex system like a school. Each member of the school community, by his/her actions, serves to enhance or impede school reform. The more members of the learning community that are committed to our goal and the means to achieve it, the higher our chances for success. While working alone in isolated classrooms may bring comfort to some, most teachers and administrators would prefer to be an active member in a vital school community. We need to create the opportunity for us to tap the talents of all on behalf of student success.

Teams and teamwork represent the engine of change in this model of continuous and sustainable school reform. Throughout this manuscript, the reader will see numerous occasions where teams and teamwork are required. The premise of the model does subscribe to the expression that *no one of us is as smart as all of us*. In the chapter on Teams, we will discuss the selection of team members, the involvement of stakeholders, and tips for developing an effective team.

Time

If one were to survey teachers and administrators around two themes, the results would be surprising. When asked informally, the vast majority of teachers and administrators say that student learning and student achievement can be improved in their school. Furthermore, many of them have a fairly clear idea of what would need to change for such improvements to occur. When asked to identify the barriers to those improvements, the most frequent response is "not enough time."

The absence of time in schools to plan and implement changes that would move the school toward higher achievement for more children is proof that the system-in-place was never designed to successfully teach all children. In reality, the absence of time is not the problem. The real problem is value choice. **Like most organizations, schools can find time for those activities that they value and can't find time for those they don't.** Therefore, the first step in creating a culture of continuous and sustainable school improvement is coming to terms with the value choices that place other activities above the need to devote quality time to the school change process.

Adjusting the value choices to provide quality time for collaborative planning for continuous improvement will not be easy. In any professional context, *time* is often a code word for *money*. If you want more time, it's going to cost someone more money. In our context, if teachers spend most of their time in front of students teaching, we'll need to extend the length of the paid day to purchase additional time when the adults can meet after the students are dismissed.

Needless to say, we will advocate a model of continuous school improvement that is as efficient as possible. However, all stakeholders will have to reach some accommodation on the time issue. Several alternative approaches to the time issue have been tried with varying degrees of success. Some proven practices will be offered later in this manuscript.

Technology

In the last several years, schools have spent billions of dollars on computer hardware, software, and connectivity. The results of this investment are not yet available. There is honest debate among concerned stakeholders as to whether schools have spent too much or too little on the "technology revolution." This debate will no doubt rage on for many years. However, few would argue that schools have done all they could or should to integrate technology into the school reform process. In far too many cases, schools have viewed computer technology as an end unto itself.

At its core, continuous improvement requires "real time" information on which to base changes. This is particularly true of schools. For example, it doesn't help for teachers and administrators to get feedback, vis-a-vis test scores, on last year's class. To be effective, teachers must know what students have learned almost immediately after teaching the lesson. That way, struggling students can quickly be identified and offered additional help. Until recently, this has been problematic. But technology has now made it possible to engage in continuous school improvement in ways that would have been unheard of even a few years ago. Students can now take an assessment on a computer and both student and teacher can have the results

almost immediately upon finishing. Technology such as this, already available in most schools, makes it possible to truly monitor and adjust instruction—a key premise in continuous improvement. This alone would take us a long way toward our goal of successful "learning for all."

Tools

Sustainable school reform, as advocated here, calls upon educators to undertake new and different work. It would be unrealistic, if not fundamentally unfair, to expect busy educators to face the challenge of the new work requirements if we did not provide the necessary tools and guidance on how to use them.

Learning to use tools is always made easier when the learning occurs within the appropriate context. So it is here. The tools will be introduced as we progress through the steps on the endless journey to sustainable school reform. Three types of quality tools are critical to successful implementation of continuous school improvement: Data Gathering, Data Analysis, and Data Display. We will give you an overview of the specific tools that have proven useful to continuous school improvement, as well as a list of resources for further exploration.

KEY CONCEPTS

Theories

- Effective Schools
- Systems Thinking
- Continuous Improvement

Teams

- Empowerment
- Consensus Building
- Problem Solving

Time

- Team Time
- Staff Development
- Study Groups

Technology

- Real Time Data
- Just-in-Time Information
- Research/Proven Practices

Tools

- Data Gathering
- Data Analysis
- Data Display

Constantly Improving Student Achievement

Chapter 2

The Effective Schools Framework

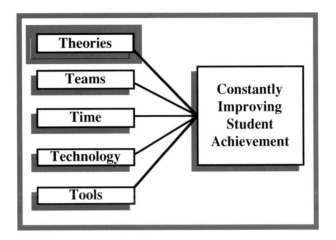

Someone once said that history is our best teacher. Let's begin our journey with an overview of the Effective Schools Movement and how it has evolved over time. It seems reasonable to refer to the Effective Schools Movement as such for several reasons. First, it has been part of the discourse on public education for well over thirty years, far longer than what others might call the latest educational fad. Second, current research continues to build upon, validate, and enrich our understanding of the original research. Third, the extent to which the research framework has been integrated into state and local policies and reform practices in virtually every state verifies that we are truly looking at an educational change of gigantic proportions.

In July 1966, "The Equal Educational Opportunity Survey" by J.S. Coleman, et al., was published. The Coleman report concluded that family background, not the school, was the major determinant of student achievement. Coleman was foremost among a group of social scientists who, during the 1960's and 70's, believed that family factors such as poverty or a parent's lack of education prevented children from learning regardless of the method of instruction. His report, along with the related literature, was the catalyst to the creation of the "compensatory education" programs that dominated school improvement throughout those decades. According to Ron Edmonds, these programs—provided chiefly through Title 1 of the Elementary-Secondary Education Act—"taught low-income children to learn in ways that conformed to most schools' preferred ways of teaching." These programs focused on changing students' behavior in order to compensate for their disadvantaged backgrounds, but made no effort to change *school behavior*. As a result, children who could not "fit" into the existing school structure—despite the school's best efforts—simply fell between the cracks.

By lending official credence to the notion that "schools didn't make a difference" in predicting student achievement, the report stimulated a vigorous reaction, instigating many of the studies that would later come to define the research base for the Effective Schools Movement. The educational researchers who conducted these studies, Wilbur Brookover, Ron Edmonds, and Larry Lezotte among them, developed a body of research that supported the premise that all children can learn and that the school controls the factors necessary to assure student mastery of the core curriculum. Of course, the Effective Schools Movement did not discount the important impact of family on student learning. In 1982, Ron Edmonds published a paper entitled "Programs of School Improvement: An Overview," in which he states "while schools may be primarily responsible for whether or not students function adequately in school, the family is probably critical in determining whether or not students *flourish* in school."

The first task of the Effective Schools Researchers was to identify existing effective schools—schools that were successful in educating all students regardless of their socioeconomic status or family background. Examples of these especially effective schools were found repeatedly, in varying locations and in both large and small communities. After identifying these schools, the task remained to identify the common characteristics among them. In other words, what philosophies, policies, and practices did these schools have in common with each other and different from their less-effective counterparts?

Upon closer inspection, the researchers found that all of these especially effective schools had strong instructional leadership, a strong sense of mission, demonstrated effective instructional behaviors, held high expectations for all students, practiced frequent monitoring of student achievement, and operated in a safe and orderly manner.

These attributes eventually became known as the Correlates of Effective Schools.

Edmonds first formally identified the Correlates of Effective Schools in the 1982 publication noted above. In this paper, Edmonds stated that all effective schools had:

- "the leadership of the principal notable for substantial attention to the quality of instruction;

- "a pervasive and broadly understood instructional focus;

- "an orderly, safe climate conducive to teaching and learning;

- "teacher behaviors that convey the expectation that all students are expected to obtain at least minimum mastery;

- "the use of measures of pupil achievement as the basis for program evaluation."

While Edmonds, Brookover, and Lezotte conducted the original effective schools research in elementary schools, another team of researchers in the United Kingdom was conducting similar research, only in secondary schools. Their independent research was published in America in 1979, in the book *Fifteen Thousand Hours* (Rutter, et al.). The conclusions they reached about school attributes that positively affect student achievement were nearly identical to those rising out of Effective Schools Research.

The results of the original research in the U.S. and Britain, plus the hundreds of subsequent research studies further confirming the attributes of an effective school, gives credence to this insightful assertion by Ron Edmonds:

> *We can, whenever and wherever we choose, successfully teach all children whose schooling is of interest to us. We already know more than we need to do that. Whether or not we do it must finally depend on how we feel about the fact that we haven't so far.*

We've come a long way since the Correlates were first published, and the research has continued to bear out these basic beliefs of the Effective Schools Movement:

- all children can learn and come to school motivated to do so;

- schools control enough of the variables to assure that virtually all students do learn;

- schools should be held accountable for measured student achievement;

- schools should disaggregate measured student achievement to be certain that students, regardless of gender, race, ethnicity, or socioeconomic status, are successfully learning the intended school curriculum;

- the internal and external stakeholders of the individual school are the most qualified and capable people to plan and implement the changes necessary to fulfill the "learning for all" mission.

The Effective Schools Movement, its constituent research, and the Correlates themselves have not only withstood the test of time, but have also evolved and grown as our understanding of effective schools has both deepened and broadened. Over the years, the Correlates have been refined and expanded to the following:

- **Instructional Leadership**
- **Clear and Focused Mission**
- **Safe and Orderly Environment**
- **Climate of High Expectations**
- **Frequent Monitoring of Student Progress**
- **Positive Home-School Relations**
- **Opportunity to Learn and Student Time on Task**

Other aspects of the Effective Schools Movement have evolved over the years as well. The early definition of effective schools rested on the concept of equity between children from differing socioeconomic classes. As educators became concerned about equity among other subsets of the population, gender, ethnicity, disabilities, and family structure were added to the mix. Furthermore, the early definition was cast in terms of mastery of essential curriculum, i.e., reading and arithmetic. Over time, other curricular outcomes were added: problem-solving ability, higher-order thinking skills, creativity, and communicative ability.

The early Effective Schools Movement also emphasized the individual school as the unit of change. While this remains the primary focus, it has become clear that school improvement resulting in increased student achievement can only be sustained with strong district support.

Finally, organizational management theories provided significant additions to Effective Schools Research and policy. The concepts of decentralization and empowerment, the importance of organizational culture, and the principles of total quality management and continuous improvement have added important dimensions to our understanding of effective schools.

A Primer on the Correlates of Effective Schools

The following descriptions are intended to give you a basic understanding of each correlate as it was first conceptualized. As you begin to successfully implement the Correlates, the question may arise, "What next?" At that point, you will be ready to consider and implement the Second-Generation Correlates—an even more challenging developmental stage for schools committed to the "learning for all" mission. A description of the Second-Generation Correlates is included in the appendix. But remember, you must walk before you run, and the original Correlates must be in place **before** your school can aspire to the next level of development.

Instructional Leadership

In the effective school, the principal acts as an instructional leader and effectively and persistently communicates the mission of the school to staff, parents, and students. In addition, the principal understands and applies the characteristics of instructional effectiveness in the management of the instructional program.

Clearly the role of the principal as the articulator of the mission of the school is crucial to the overall effectiveness of the school. If you read *In Search of Excellence*, the management bible written by Tom Peters and Bob Waterman, you'll quickly discover that complex organizations, like schools, suffer from drift with respect to the core values or mission. They emphasize that it is the obligation of the leader to make sure that everyone has a shared sense of purpose, and a shared understanding of the mission and core values of the organization. Clearly, schools qualify as complex organizations that require strong leadership. The principal must fulfill this role.

> *There may be schools out there that have strong instructional leaders, but are not yet effective; however, we have never yet found an effective school that did not have a strong instructional leader as the principal.*
>
> — Ron Edmonds

Clear and Focused Mission

In the effective school, there is a clearly articulated mission of the school through which the staff shares an understanding of and a commitment to the school's goals, priorities, assessment procedures, and accountability. The staff in the effective school accepts responsibility for the students' learning of the essential curricular goals.

When we first started doing research on effective schools, we took as a given that schools had a shared understanding of what their mission was and ought to be. The more we work with schools and the more we visit a variety of schools, the more we become convinced that the issue of mission is one that must receive substantial discussion.

When you think about all the things that might be done in the name of good education and realize the limits of your time, people power, and organizational energy, it becomes clear that there has to be some focus to the overall effort. This idea of a shared sense of mission is one way to assure that we're all moving in the same direction. One way to ascertain whether your school has a clear focus is to ask each stakeholder "What does this school care most about?" Would you get the same answer from each individual asked, or many different answers? To the extent that there are many answers, the school would be said to lack a shared sense of mission.

Safe and Orderly Environment

In the effective school, we say there is an orderly, purposeful, business-like atmosphere, which is free from the threat of physical harm. The school climate is not oppressive and is conducive to teaching and learning.

For many years, parents have said that the safety and disciplinary climate of the school is their first concern when judging schools. School shootings, bomb scares, and other senseless violent acts have only served to deepen parental concerns. Obviously, the learning environment must be a safe and secure place for our children's sake.

We also want schools to be safe and secure because the presence or absence of a safe learning environment enhances or impedes learning. Even if the environment does not sink to the level of shootings or bomb scares, the extent to which student learning is interrupted by routine disciplinary problems serves to diminish learning. Therefore, the goal of the effective school is to minimize, if not totally eliminate, such incidents.

A safe and orderly environment is one of the easier correlates to address if you can get certain conditions in place.

First, all the adults, but most particularly teachers, must accept that *they are on duty, all the time, everywhere, during school hours.* If there's a place in the school or a time in the day when students perceive that there is no adult on duty, that's my nomination for a trouble spot. Second, rules must be enforced with absolute consistency across all teachers and administrators in the school. Inconsistency will quickly undercut and destroy the orderly environment of a school. Students will be quick to pick up on inconsistent enforcement and be quick to cry "unfair." Quite frankly, they're right.

Student academic and social engagement in school is another factor to be addressed in the general learning climate. Research shows that strong student engagement is important all along the learning path, but becomes especially significant at the middle and high school levels.

Climate of High Expectations

In the effective school, there is a climate of high expectations in which the staff believes and demonstrates that all students can obtain mastery of the school's essential curriculum. They also believe that they, the staff, have the capability to help all students obtain that mastery.

What are some of the important implied notions in the High Expectations for Success Correlate? I'd like to emphasize the words **for success** in the description because there are an awful

> *The finest gift we can give our children is our heartfelt belief that they can succeed.*
>
> — Lawrence W. Lezotte

lot of people who believe that simply raising the standards in a school communicates higher expectations to students. In Reality, there is a world of difference between high standards and high expectations. High standards are those externalities that we ask students to meet, i.e., graduation requirements. Expectations reflect the internal belief systems of the adults in the schools. High achieving schools have a Climate of High Expectations where teachers believe that kids can and will meet those higher standards. Expectations are crucial.

Frequent Monitoring of Student Progress

In the effective school, pupil progress over the essential objectives are measured frequently, monitored frequently, and the results of those assessments are used to improve the individual student behaviors and performances, as well as to improve the curriculum as a whole.

How often should student progress be monitored? The answer depends on how frequently you are prepared to adjust your instruction. If you don't ever intend to adjust instruction, then why bother monitoring at all? The only justification for monitoring without adjusting is if your mission is primarily one of sorting and selecting students. And if that is the case, assessment becomes a way to keep disadvantaged students in lower-level tracks.

Frequent Monitoring of Student Progress—one of the most important and yet misunderstood of the Correlates—means much more than just state standardized tests. While state tests are a fact of life and will soon be expanded to more children in more grades, they are of little help in improving individual student learning. This is because the results of these assessments usually do not get back to the school in time to be of much use in identifying and helping struggling students. Schools that seek higher achievement will embrace this correlate, using frequent monitoring as a tool to help all children master the essential curriculum. These schools will then make the transition from teaching-centered organizations to proactive, learner-centered educational communities.

Positive Home-School Relations

In the effective school, parents understand and support the basic mission of the school and are given opportunities to play important roles in helping the school to achieve its mission.

It's possible for schools to be effective in having the students master the basic skills curriculum without extraordinary levels of parent involvement and support. But it is much easier if parents are part of the collaborative team and are seen by the school as partners in the education of their youngsters. That's a much more difficult task today because of our mobile society, the increase in two-career and single-parent families, as well as families who speak little or no English. The distances some children travel to school also complicate matters.

Involving parents in the school improvement process can be challenging, particularly in schools where there is a high level of poverty and/or non-English speaking families. This is where our mental models can interfere with the successful involvement of these parents. Teachers and administrators must suspend their assumptions about the interest and ability of their students' parents and make an earnest effort to include them in the process. This may take one—or many—special efforts to provide a variety of opportunities for parent involvement. Parents may need training in how to participate, both at home with their children and at school. Parents, in turn, must set aside their assumptions about the school, its faculty, and their views about their own abilities so they can contribute to the process and to their children's education.

Opportunity to Learn and Student Time on Task

In the effective school, teachers allocate a significant amount of classroom time to instruction in the essential curricular areas. For a high percentage of this time, students are actively engaged in whole-class or large group, teacher-directed, planned learning activities.

This simply says that kids tend to learn most things that they spend time on. If you want your students to master certain curricular objectives and goals, one of the first prerequisites is to assure that they spend time on them. We see instance after instance where students are held accountable for outcomes over which they were never taught. This is patently unfair and must be changed.

The 7 Correlates of Effective Schools

Instructional Leadership

Clear and Focused Mission

Safe and Orderly Environment

Climate of High Expectations

Frequent Monitoring of Student Progress

Positive Home-School Relations

Opportunity to Learn and Student Time on Task

The Correlates of Effective Schools provide school improvement teams with a comprehensive framework for identifying, categorizing, and solving the problems that schools and school districts face. And because the Correlates are based upon the documented successes of effective schools, they offer hope and inspiration to those struggling to improve. **If the schools from which the Correlates are drawn can do it, SO CAN YOU!**

Figure 2.1

Time on task implies that each of the teachers in the school has a clear understanding of what the essential learner objectives are, grade-by-grade and subject-by-subject. Once we are clear on what students should be learning, students must be given the time to learn it. This can be tricky because interruptions in the day-to-day flow of routines in the classroom and in the schools seriously and significantly detract from our ability to be effective for all of our kids.

Defining the Effective School

What is meant by the term Effective School? We are all well aware of the importance of carefully selecting and defining our terms. Therefore, some time will be devoted to explaining the philosophical and conceptual basis for the terms **Effective School** and **Improving School**.

From the earliest writings of our founding fathers, the vision for the United States generally, and its public schools specifically, has rested on the two value pillars of *quality* and *equity*. Diane Ravitch, educational historian and scholar, stated it well when she said that in a democracy there must be an indissoluble link between quality and equity. She goes on to say that if a democracy chooses to ignore issues of either quality or equity, in time the democracy will fail.

Peter Drucker, noted management scholar and author, defines "effective" as doing the right job. Given the vision of our founding fathers, the right job for public education centers around the

simultaneous pursuit of quality and equity.

> Quality and equity must therefore be the two uncompromising aims of every public school in America. We must ensure that every child has access to a quality education and that each child has an equal educational opportunity.

Two assumptions are key to this philosophy and the definitional framework of the Effective School. First, we associate the level of measured achievement with the dimension of quality. Second, we associate the distribution of measured achievement across subsets of the student population with the dimension of educational equity.

Within this context, let us now offer a definition for an Effective School:

An Effective School is a school that can, in measured student achievement terms, demonstrate the joint presence of quality and equity. Said another way, an Effective School is a school that can, in measured student achievement terms and reflective of its "learning for all" mission, demonstrate high overall levels of achievement and no gaps in the distribution of that achievement across major subsets of the student population.

Schools that meet these standards, while still in the minority, do exist. Their existence removes the concept of the Effective School from the realm of the conceptual and brings it into the realm of reality. However, the vast majority of our schools are still somewhere along the continuum of effectiveness.

How do we define an Improving School based on this definition of the Effective School?

An improving school is a school that can, in measured student achievement reflective of its "learning for all" mission, demonstrate the increasing presence of both quality and equity.

One way to simplify the distinction between an Effective School and an Improving School would be to note the following. By definition, an Effective School has already arrived—met the goals of quality and equity. An Improving School is a school that is trending toward effectiveness, but has not yet arrived. Note that the definition of an improving school is not based on how well a school is doing compared to other schools. Although we find joy in celebrating an effective school whenever and wherever we find one, the core of the sustainable and continuous school reform model offered here emphasizes improvement. This emphasis requires a school to use its own trend data as the primary basis for assessing improvement over time. By measuring progress against a previous benchmark, a school can avoid the temptation to engage in counterproductive normative comparisons with other schools.

Now that you know the history and definition of the Effective School, and have had an introduction to the Correlates of Effective Schools as

reported in the literature, it's time to elaborate on the issues of evidence for either school effectiveness or school improvement.

Evidence of Effectiveness

Having defined the Effective School, we turn to the question of evidence. What will we accept as evidence of high educational attainment? First and foremost, we will look at educational attainment as reflected in a variety of output measures, including state assessment scores, other achievement test results, graduation rates, and any other output indicators that are recommended by legitimate stakeholders. We will also be attentive to other dimensions, namely inputs, process and program indicators, as well as safety, orderliness, and discipline.

> However, no school or district can be judged as effective, regardless of the input or process evidence, if it cannot demonstrate high student achievement in the essential curriculum as reflected in output measures without major gaps in the distribution of achievement across the various student groups.

Because of the current achievement gaps facing public education, three subsets of the pupil population should receive immediate consideration. They are gender, race or ethnicity, and socioeconomic status. We emphasize these three dimensions because they constitute the major predictors of observed gaps in measured student achievement. As a matter of fact, the relative importance of the three variables is the reverse order of their listing. Socioeconomic status is still the single strongest predictor of student achievement in most schools in America.

The key, then, to demonstrating high levels of educational attainment is to describe, in observable and measurable terms, the specific student outcomes we want.

The Correlates as Leading Indicators

The standards, assessment, and accountability movement of the last decade has virtually everyone—teachers, administrators, policymakers, and parents—focusing on measured student achievement. The focus on measured student achievement has been, is now, and long will be, the object of many heated debates among the various stakeholders. Our goal here is not to weigh-in on the goodness or badness, rightness or wrongness of this focus. Our goal here is to see how and where this emphasis fits into continuous and sustainable school improvement.

By the definition presented earlier, we have already established that an effective school earns and maintains that status by virtue of the level and distribution of measured student achievement on assessments that reflect the learning mission of the school. Unfortunately, if you have a role in school improvement you will discover, if you haven't already, that school achievement results are of limited value if you want to develop a plan to improve the school.

The reason for this disappointing discovery is due to the fact that measured student achievement is what the economist would call a "trailing indicator"; it is an "after-the-fact" measure of learning. According to economists and systems theorists, you can't improve the quality of the system very much by simply focusing on the trailing indicators (outputs) of the system. Make no mistake, the trailing indicators of measured student achievement are vital to assessing effectiveness and degree of improvement; they are, however, extremely limited in how much they can help you change the system.

This fact is beginning to be recognized by educational researchers and those responsible for staff development and school improvement. As noted researcher Rhona Weinstein states, "School-based interventions that focus only on end-point student outcomes will always miss an important part of the intervention impact. Clearly, important program effects reside at multiple levels, such as in teachers' beliefs and actions, the development of school policy, and school climate, in addition to changed student behavior." (Weinstein, Rhona S. et al., 1983)

To significantly impact the trailing indicators or outputs (in this case, student performance), you must focus on the **leading indicators** that cause, or at least significantly influence, the trailing indicators. Therefore, a second domain of information would need to capture these leading indicators, specifically the critical aspects of the teaching/learning environment known to impact student learning.

The Correlates are critical to the effective school because they represent the leading organizational and contextual indicators that have been shown to influence student learning. In other words, **the extent to which the Correlates are in place in a school has a dramatic, positive effect on student achievement.** Furthermore, the individual correlates are not independent of one another, but are interdependent. For example, discipline problems in the learning environment relate to the safety and orderliness of the learning environment as well as the opportunity to learn and time on task.

Later in this text we will discuss the tools that will assist you in monitoring the presence of the Correlates in your school or district through the use of leading indicators.

KEY CONCEPTS

- Research has shown that schools do indeed have the ability to assure that virtually all students master the essential curriculum. **Schools do make a difference!**

- The Effective School can demonstrate both **quality** and **equity**: high student achievement for all students, regardless of race, gender, or socioeconomic status.

- The **Correlates of Effective Schools** are the characteristics that have been found, through over 30 years of school improvement research, to be typical of effective schools. They include:

     Instructional Leadership
     Clear and Focused Mission
     Safe and Orderly Environment
     Climate of High Expectations
     Frequent Monitoring of Student Progress
     Positive Home-School Relations
     Opportunity to Learn and Student Time on Task

- While student outcomes or **trailing indicators** provide the ultimate evidence of school effectiveness, the Correlates provide the **leading indicators** for those critical factors that influence student achievement.

Chapter 3

Systems Theory

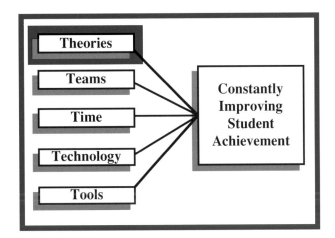

Systems Theory represents a body of scholarly writings and empirical studies that have been widely read, discussed, and proven useful in understanding how and why things happen as they do. Systems Theory can help in planning sustainable change in complex organizations. Unfortunately, the preparation programs for most teachers and administrators do not explicitly include this body of knowledge. Systems Theory and many of its key concepts are integrated into this comprehensive approach to sustainable school reform.

Defining a System

For our purposes, we will define a system as a network of interdependent components that work together to accomplish the aim of the system. Let us attempt to place this deceptively simple definition in the context of education.

An educational system is a network of interdependent processes and procedures that work together to accomplish the aim of the system: producing an educated citizen. In its broadest context, the education system for the individual is much larger than formal schooling; however, we will focus on formal schooling and that component known as the school itself.

Describing the System-in-Place

Systems scholar Patrick Dolan uses the term "system-in-place" as a convenient and descriptive phrase to describe the system that is. It is important for anyone who would seek to reform the education system in general, and the school in particular, to have an appreciation for the system-in-place. To ignore the system-in-place and equate school reform with simply a call to ask teachers or principals to work harder and care more, is doomed to failure from the outset.

What are some of the critical elements of the public schooling system to keep in mind in planning sustainable reform?

- **Public education is a classic top-down bureaucracy.**

In Dolan's terms, public education represents a "command and control" system. In such systems, the authority rests at the top of the system and the accountability and responsibility rests at the bottom. In the context of public education, the State has the authority for public education, as set forth in the U.S. Constitution; teachers and schools are accountable for student learning.

- **Public education is a deeply layered system.**

The system of public education has students nested in classrooms, classrooms nested in schools, schools nested in school districts, and districts organized by state. These nests can serve as a major barricade to the flow of information from the top down or from the bottom up. For example, in their zeal to reform schools, most states have adopted and mandated a core curriculum for their schools. However, if this curriculum is going to affect student achievement, it must penetrate every barrier and truly change what students are taught in the classroom.

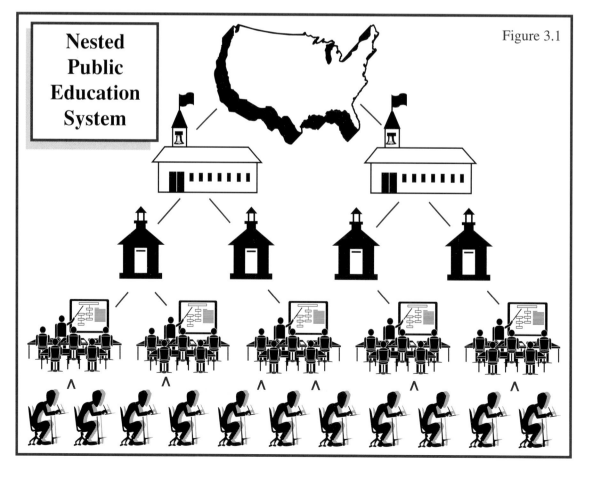

Nested Public Education System

Figure 3.1

- **Public education has an enormous amount of inertia to keep doing what it has always done.**

One of the strengths of a classic bureaucratic system is that once it is up and running and the culture is set, it can be virtually left alone for a thousand years and it probably would not change. Clearly this predictability and inertia represents a real asset—providing the system is doing what you want it to do. Unfortunately, the inertia of the system-in-place turns out to be its greatest liability if we want the system to do something different. Sustainable school reform requires that schools do something different and thus faces the challenge of overcoming the inertia.

- **Public education, like other systems, strives to maintain balance in the status quo and doesn't easily embrace change.**

The human body is a complex system that strives to maintain balance in the healthy status quo. The components of the system send signals when we need to drink more water, take in food, get rest, and so on. The human body also has an elaborate immune system. This particular system strives to seek and destroy invaders of all sorts seeking to change the system. Usually, the immune system's behavior is not only good, but essential for our very survival. However, the immune system itself can become a threat to our survival when it wrongly perceives a change—such as an organ transplant—as something to be rejected.

Public education, like the human system, is a complex system with many mechanisms designed to maintain the healthy status quo. Similarly, it also has an "immune system" that watches for those unwelcome invaders trying to invoke change. By continuing to look at fundamental change as a disruption or threat instead of an opportunity to "get well," public education is truly at risk of destroying itself.

- **The system of public education, like other systems, is held in place by anchors.**

We are all familiar with a circus tent. While the tent is obvious, it is easy to overlook the fact that the tent is held in place by anchoring ropes. If we liken the tent to the education system, the ropes are the stakeholders that hold the system in place. If we wish to change the location of the circus tent, we must begin the change process with the ropes that are holding it in place. Likewise, if we are interested in sustainable reform of the public education system, we must begin with the anchors—the stakeholders—holding the system in place.

Who are the anchors that hold the system of public education in place? The local school board, and the community it represents, constitutes a broad group of anchors to the system-in-place. In addition, school administrators—the aristocrats of the current system—have a vested interest in the system-in-place. Teachers, and the associations and unions who represent them, also have a stake in the system-in-place. Students, noncertified employees, cooks, custodians, and bus drivers would likely feel the impact of any change in the system-in-place. **To create sustainable change in the system-in-place, the permission and support of the stakeholder groups is essential.**

Systems Theory: Principles and Concepts

Other concepts and principles found in the systems theory literature can help create sustainable reform for public education. The discussion presented below is selective and in no way claims to be exhaustive of all the potentially useful systems concepts and principles. Each of the concepts and principles will be discussed in the context of our general discussion of sustainable and continuous improvement of the educational system.

Mental Models

Most adults and children carry with them an internalized schema or mental image of what a school is, what's good or bad about schools, and what would constitute improvement of a school. These mental models are based on an individual's personal experiences and are deeply rooted in the past. They consist of the "images, assumptions, and stories that we carry in our minds" that serve as the basis of an individual's behavior. (Senge, 2001) Said another way, our mental models become our "theory-in-use."

Mental models of public education are both good and bad. On the good side, the fact that nearly everyone has had experience with public schools means that reformers don't have to spend a lot of time teaching them about the topic. Now for the bad news: mental models filter what we see and believe based on our assumptions about and experiences with public education. We are usually not even aware of the mental model from which we are operating. According to Peter Senge, in *Schools That Learn*, this causes some of the most difficult challenges for school reform:

Mental models thus limit people's ability to change. A group of superintendents and school board members may tacitly believe that the only way to improve the schools is to invest more money; therefore, they don't recognize other possible approaches. A teacher may assume that students from the "wrong side of the tracks" don't care about school, so he subtly dismisses them out of hand. An administrator may assume that the local teachers' union will block all innovation, so she approaches the unions defensively, holding back as much information as possible—which in turn makes the union leaders more defensive. The leaders of a school reform effort may assume, without even being fully aware of it, that parents don't really know much about their children's needs. Therefore, they inadvertently alienate parent groups, without ever understanding why. A forty-five year old laborer who never earned a high school diploma may assume that his children's teachers look down on him; he never summons the courage to come in to the school for meetings and the teachers assume he doesn't care. A local community member may assume that, because many schoolteachers are women, they do not need to be paid as much—and vote down the school referendum.

As a result of their mental models, there may be little or no agreement among stakeholders as to what needs to change or what would constitute evidence of improvement.

How do we deal with mental models? According to Senge, we must cultivate two skills: **reflection** and **inquiry**. We must be willing to examine our own mental models (reflection) and to engage in meaningful dialog with others in a way that identifies and clarifies the underlying assumptions of everyone involved in the school reform process (inquiry). In this way, all stakeholders can reach a consensus about "what is" and "what ought to be."

Double Loop Learning Model

Noted systems scholar Gareth Morgan, in his best selling book *Images of Organization,* introduces us to what he calls the Double Loop Learning Model. Single loop learning, according to Morgan, consists of the tactics,

strategies, and behaviors that the system employs to achieve its mission and its monitoring of the organization's performance against existing norms to keep it "on track." Single loop learning reinforces the status quo because there is no avenue within this model for questioning the norms or paradigm under which the organization operates. Bureaucratic structures—such as the deeply layered public school system—reinforce single loop learning by restricting the free flow of information throughout the entire system.

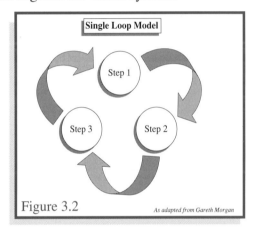

Figure 3.2 — *As adapted from Gareth Morgan*

Double loop learning adds another dimension to organizational learning. This second loop represents the process of reviewing the relevance and the usefulness of the norms, core beliefs, and core values that frame the organization's behaviors and changing them where necessary.

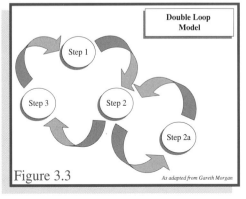

Figure 3.3 — *As adapted from Gareth Morgan*

Where does this concept fit into our discussion of continuous and sustainable school reform? The accountability movement of the last decade and the newest federal legislation have placed ever-increasing pressure on educators for higher student achievement. In response, educators have focused on the first loop, looking for the newest and best programs, and have been reluctant to explore the core beliefs and values that underpin the American public education system. In fact, according to Morgan, bureaucratic accountability and their systems of rewards and punishment (such as sanctions against failing schools) can actually create barriers to double loop learning. This is because people, such as school staff members, who feel threatened or vulnerable often engage in "defensive routines."

At the extreme, these defensive routines can become entrenched in the organization's culture and result in highly resistant organizations that use job descriptions, rigid rules, and other structural elements to reinforce the status quo. Such schools may institute new programs and technologies, but they will have little effect on student achievement. It is clear from Morgan's model that schools must step away from this defensive posture and engage in authentic dialog that leads to an honest review of the mission, core values, and core beliefs. Schools must also be willing to make fundamental changes in these areas; otherwise, changes in the school's strategies, tactics, and behaviors will not be sustainable.

If Gareth Morgan is right, school reform will not be found in the newest "silver bullet" program. Sustainable educational reforms will only be realized when the core beliefs and values of the system in place are explored and, where necessary, changed. In later sections of this manuscript, we will present some tools that will help you facilitate the process of clarifying your school's mission, core beliefs, and core values.

Two additional principles of Systems Theory are key to continuous school improvement: the principles of prevention and response.

Prevention Principle

The most cost-effective and efficient way to solve a problem is to prevent it in the first place. Total quality systems are deeply committed to the prevention principle. They easily demonstrate that the more resources an organization must use to solve problems, the fewer resources it has for other purposes. The most effective way to free resources, then, would be to prevent problems before they occur.

Public schools, as a rule, do not value prevention. As a matter of fact, public schools would lose money if they prevented learning problems since a great deal of funding is allocated based on their existence. Much of the new money and new programs that have come into education in the last 25 years or so have been designed to "back-load" failure rather than "front-load" success. Make no mistake—this principle should not be interpreted to mean that we need less money in public education. The prevention principle suggests that resources should be made available for schools so they can prevent learning problems. This is because, when it comes to learning, we know a lot more about how to teach it right the first time than we know about how to teach it over once we've failed.

The prevention principle must become one of the core values of public education. There is extensive research that identifies successful prevention strategies. Teachers themselves are adept at recognizing potential problems. However, public schools lack any systematic procedures for identifying potential learning problems and implementing the steps necessary to prevent them. Administrators and teachers must work together to identify and prevent these problems.

Responsive Principle

The prevention principle calls organizations to solve all problems before they even occur. The responsive principle is its companion. It states that if you cannot solve a problem before it occurs, at least solve it **as soon as it occurs**. Here again, schools seem to ignore this opportunity. For example, most teachers have a pretty good idea which students are likely to fail to master the intended curriculum for a given year by about the third week of school. Unfortunately, help does not come for those failing students until the end of the semester, or maybe even the end of the school year, when the students are retained and recycled.

Manufacturing companies in the private sector have developed just-in-time inventory systems. Such systems

have proven to be very efficient and effective in that they save the company millions of dollars and the customer precious time. The effective school needs to borrow this just-in-time idea and incorporate a **just-in-time intervention system**. In the new system, the length of time the learner flounders before help comes would be a matter of minutes—not weeks or months. **Help comes immediately and in sufficient quantity and quality to, effectively and efficiently, assist the learner in meeting the instructional objective**. This is critical because our ability to solve student learning problems is greatest at the point when the problem is first identified. The evidence is clear that if students linger in failure and frustration for any length of time, the prospect of reclaiming those students goes down quickly.

To illustrate this concept, suppose that a group of students had met the prerequisites for the new learning. The teacher delivers the new lesson, and immediately assesses student performance. The results show that several students failed to meet the expected performance standard. At this point, we need data that will help us understand why these particular students failed. If we know about the actual experiences the learners encountered during the lesson, we may be able solve the problem for those learners immediately and prevent it for future learners. Immediate deployment of mentors and coaches and extended time on task are just two examples of how a just-in-time intervention system might work.

Clearly, the promise of the prevention and responsive principles is great. Unfortunately, successful implementation of these principles will require systemic changes that will not be easy and are bound to be resisted by many both in and outside the schools. The payoff is going to be worth the effort, however, as we move closer to our mission of "learning for all."

Changing the System

Peter Senge, systems theory expert, identifies 11 laws of systems theory in his book, *The Fifth Discipline*. The 11th law is "There is no blame." Senge states, "We tend to blame outside circumstances for our problems. . . . Systems thinking shows us that there is no outside; that you and the cause of your problems are part of a single system." Given this concept, we offer the core belief upon which this reform model rests:

You and your colleagues are already doing the best you know how to do, given the conditions in which you find yourself.

If we accept this belief as true, and we want to change the results we've been getting, three conditions must be met:

- The mission, core values, and core beliefs must be reviewed and changed if necessary to reflect the current reality in which the school finds itself.

- New knowledge must be brought into the system.

- The structure of the system itself must be changed to reflect the revised mission, core values, and core beliefs. (See figure on page 33.)

If your plan of action does not address these key issues, it is unlikely you will make any lasting change in student achievement.

To help you synthesize these ideas into a cogent and useful framework, we have adapted Gareth Morgan's model of Double Loop Learning to incorporate the influence of the changing educational context and the new knowledge that is needed to effectively respond to these changes.

> *Systemic forces will win out over the most noble vision if we do not learn how to recognize, work with, and gently mold these forces.*
>
> — Peter Senge

Figure 3.4

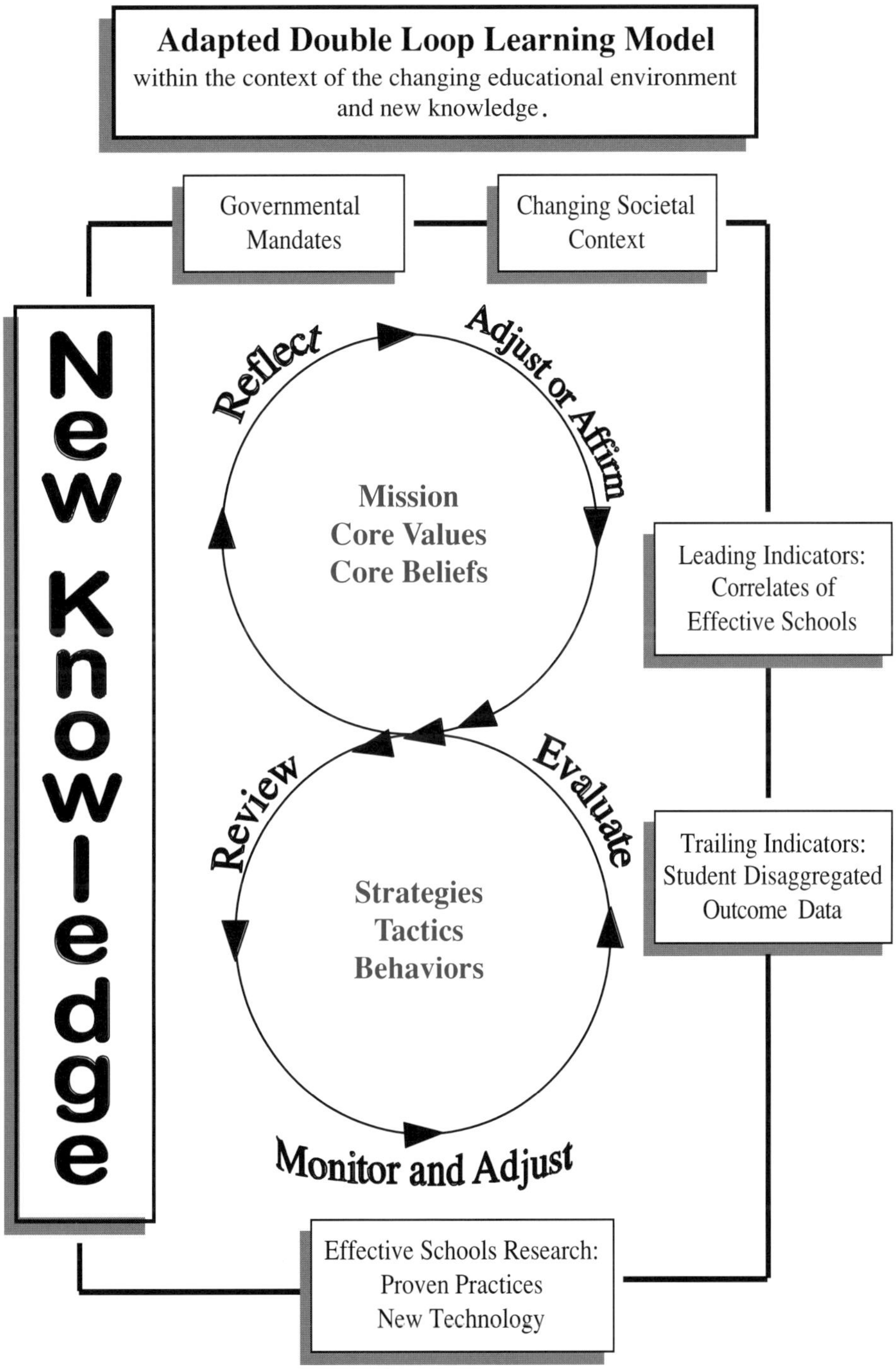

Adapted Double Loop Learning Model
within the context of the changing educational environment
and new knowledge.

Governmental Mandates

Changing Societal Context

New Knowledge

Reflect

Adjust or Affirm

Mission
Core Values
Core Beliefs

Leading Indicators:
Correlates of
Effective Schools

Review

Evaluate

Strategies
Tactics
Behaviors

Trailing Indicators:
Student Disaggregated
Outcome Data

Monitor and Adjust

Effective Schools Research:
Proven Practices
New Technology

Examples of questions to ask about mission, core beliefs, and core values:

- What do we believe?
- Do our core beliefs and values support the stated mission?
- Does our mission reflect the current input of all relevant stakeholders?
- Does our mission specify what learner outcomes are important to us and who is accountable for those outcomes?
- Are current strategies, tactics, and behaviors consistent with the current mission, core beliefs, and core values?

KEY CONCEPTS

Definition of a System. A system is a network of interdependent processes and procedures that work together to accomplish the aim of the system. The aim of public education has changed from mandatory attendance to mandatory learning. The system of public education has been slow to reflect that change in mission.

Sustainable change requires that . . .

- We have a realistic and accurate idea of the system-in-place.

- The mission, core values, and core beliefs be reviewed and revised to reflect the current reality of public education: "learning for all."

- New knowledge be brought into the system.

- All relevant stakeholders be involved in the process.

- Structural and procedural changes are consistent with the revised mission, beliefs, and values.

- Individuals involved in the process be willing to examine their own mental models and be aware of preconceived notions.

Prevention and Responsive Principles. The total quality effective school must embrace the twin values of prevention and immediate response when it comes to learning problems. This means:

- Teach it right the first time, based on proven practices.

- Adopt a **just-in-time intervention system**: continuous monitoring of student performance and adjusting of instruction to meet the needs of struggling students.

Chapter 4

Continuous Improvement Theory

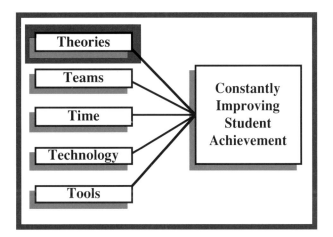

Continuous improvement is both an attitude and a set of concepts and tools. The underlying attitude is that anything and everything can be improved. There are a couple of different ways that this attitude has been used to describe school improvement. In this context, school improvement may be thought of as a good news, bad news message. The good news is that school improvement can begin anytime. The bad news is that you are never finished with school improvement. School improvement is an endless succession of incremental adjustments.

Because of these underlying beliefs, certain assumptions become critical:

- There is room for improvement in every school. No school is, nor should it be, immune from school improvement. School improvement must not be limited to low-performing schools.

- The particular aims and goals of school improvement are unique to a single school. School improvement is most successful when it is allowed to occur school by school and one school at a time.

- The district office has an important role to play in supporting school-by-school improvement.

- Every school begins the journey somewhere on the road to school improvement and, given their current place, should set incremental goals and "next steps."

Continuous improvement can be applied to any endeavor. While we are restricting our discussion to the general topic of school improvement, this mindset could be applied to one's health and well being, one's golf game, one's lawn, and even world peace. Once the continuous improvement mindset has been internalized, individuals and organizations will never be able to look at their reality in the same way. Once you put on the glasses of continuous improvement, you'll be both amazed and frustrated by the number of targets for improvement you'll see in your everyday activities, like going to the grocery store, participating in a community event, or attending a movie.

The continuous improvement mindset presents a paradox that you must be prepared to confront as you begin the journey of school reform: the more you improve your school, the more you'll see the need for more improvement. This paradox requires schools to embrace the twin values of **patience** and **persistence**. Patience, because there are no quick fixes, and persistence, because change is never easy.

The Continuous Improvement Cycle

It is one thing to adopt a mindset that says that everything can be improved and that as educators we have a professional—even moral obligation—to pursue this improvement. It is another to convert that mindset into a set of actions that will actually result in continuous improvement. The primary tool that we will use is what is called the Continuous Improvement Cycle, which is also known as the Shewhart Cycle. In his writings, W. Edwards Deming credited Shewhart with this deceptively simple set of steps that are the mantra for continuous improvement.

In its original description, Shewhart spoke about the cycle as **Plan-Do-Check-Act**. Most people that are familiar with continuous improvement describe it in the same sequence. However, because we are using this important concept in the context of school improvement, we are going to modify the sequence slightly to flow in the following way:

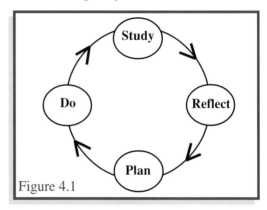

Figure 4.1

Why the change?

Consider the following analogy. Assume our mission or aim is to fly to Los Angeles. Do we file a flight plan that would have us fly north, south, east, or west? The answer is "yes" *depending on where you start*. Continuous and sustainable school improvement implies that the school already exists, has an aim or mission, and is somewhere on the journey to that aim. Before a school decides what changes are needed, it must ascertain, through careful **study,** where it is at on this journey. This may seem obvious, but this step is often ignored. This then results in choosing a strategy or solution that either solves a problem different than ours or doesn't solve any problem at all. Schools are prone to seeking a new program as the solution to every learning problem in the school.

More often than not, new programs are not the answer. This "new program trap" can be avoided if we first study the situation as it now exists.

Our goal in this step is to develop hypotheses to get to the "root cause" of the problem. For example, let's suppose that we have examined reading achievement and found that several students haven't performed well. Our first impulse might be to implement a new reading program. Upon further study, we find that those who performed poorly missed a great deal of school. We can now identify attendance as one of the root causes of low reading achievement in our school. We then can realize that, for these children, adopting a new reading program is probably not going to help unless we address the attendance problem.

This step in the cycle is to **reflect** on what we learned in the first step where we framed the problem. Part of the reflection step is exploring the research and proven practices that relate to our situation. This is especially important because policymakers are asking schools to develop school improvement plans that are research-based. Practically, it helps us avoid wasting time "reinventing the wheel."

The study phase has provided us with a description of the problem we are going to address and taken us to the root cause of that problem. In the reflection phase, we have incorporated an external scanning process to draw upon available research and proven practices and strategies. Using our attendance example, let's assume that the review of research and proven practice literature reveals that attendance problems are reduced if

schools focus on three strategies. We can now move onto the **plan** phase of the cycle.

In the plan phase, the school develops an implementation plan for the school. The plan identifies training needs, selects time lines, and develops a strategy for monitoring implementation and evaluating the overall impact of the action plan.

The fourth phase is to actually **do** or implement the plan of action and collect the designated impact data. Completion of this phase brings us full circle and we are now back to studying the data, framing a new or modified version of the problem. The continuous improvement cycle begins again. When do we stop using this mindset? **Never**!

In a later section of this manuscript, we will present and discuss specific tools and processes that can be used with each phase of the continuous improvement cycle. The most important point to be taken from this discussion is that continuous improvement is a mindset and can be used to improve any and every aspect of a school.

Continuous Improvement Concepts

Here are some other basic concepts of Continuous Improvement Theory that will prove helpful in achieving continuous and sustainable school reform.

Benchmarking

School improvement is always relative. As evidence of improvement, we can use our past accomplishments as the "benchmark" against which we compare our current achievements. This form of benchmarking relies heavily on **trend data**. Some of the specific tools that are presented in the next section will show how this type of benchmarking can be routinely done.

Benchmarking a school's progress against its own past accomplishments— **criterion-referenced benchmarking**—is consistent with the notion that school improvement occurs school-by-school, and one school at a time. However, many state accountability systems insist on benchmarking schools **normatively**. They want to know how a school is doing **relative to other schools**: all schools in the state, schools that serve similar populations, or even the highest performing schools in the state, nation, or the world (e.g. World Class Schools).

Normative benchmarking, like that suggested above, represents a perfectly

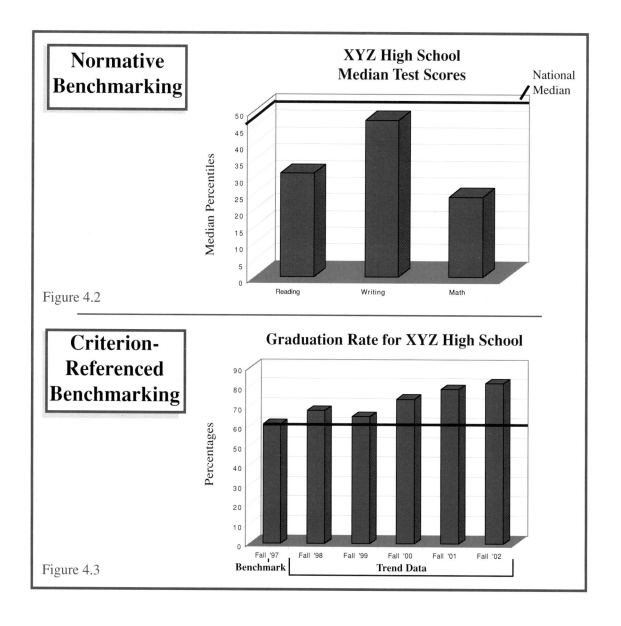

Figure 4.2

Figure 4.3

valid application of the concept. The question is *Do such comparisons serve to positively energize school improvement or simply promote despair, name calling and excuse making?* We believe that while there is a place for normative benchmarking, it should be used with caution—and never without the school's trend data being examined as well. The preponderance of the time, effort, and energy in benchmarking should focus on the question *Are we doing better in our school now than we were doing before?*

Most of the data examination that is going on in the name of school improvement looks at test scores or the **trailing indicators of learning**. As we mentioned earlier, as important as the trailing indicators are in the scheme of things, they are of limited use in informing school improvement. Repeatedly standing on the scale does not give us much help in our goal to lose weight. If we are serious about weight loss, we need to monitor diet, exercise, and other habits that are the **leading indicators**. In subsequent sections, we will use the concept of benchmarking trend data around the **leading indicators of learning**.

Measures of Central Tendency and Variability

School reformers who adopt the continuous improvement mindset will be introduced to the "wonderful world of variability" in a very big way. In the context of school reform, the concepts of **variance** and **variability** represent a radical change in thinking for many educators. The organizational culture of education tends to use measures of **central tendency** to describe student, school, or district data. When we use phrases like *average class size, average teacher salary, median test scores, or percentile ranking,* we are talking about central tendency of a distribution. However, we must remember that, for each of those descriptions, there is variability around those averages. For example, some classes are larger than the reported average and some are smaller.

One of the most powerful techniques for focusing the school reform discussion beyond measures of central tendency is to ask teachers and administrators to think about the students who fall in the bottom third of their achievement distribution. We ask them to hypothesize why these students fall in the bottom third and what would have to change for those students to perform better. Once we engage that conversation, we are on a productive path toward sustainable school reform.

One of the most important goals for school reform in America today is that of closing the gap in measured student achievement between minority and nonminority students, between middle-class and disadvantaged students. Another way to describe the goal of closing the gap is to say that we are interested in reducing, and eventually eliminating, that portion of the variability in measured student achievement that is directly traceable to social class or race.

Here is a difficult concept for many to grasp. If we were to eliminate the current gap in measured achievement between middle-class and poor

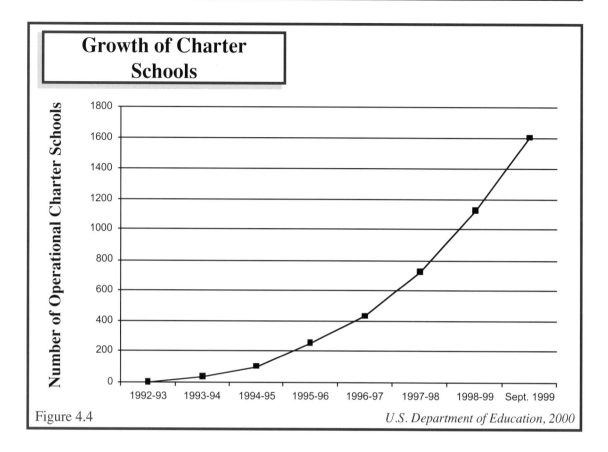

Growth of Charter Schools

Figure 4.4

U.S. Department of Education, 2000

children, would we eliminate all the individual differences in achievement? **No**. Some poor children would still achieve at a much higher level than other poor children and some middle-class children would achieve much higher than other middle-class children. *In closing the gap, we are seeking to eliminate those differences that are attributable to group membership.*

There are tremendous benefits to thoughtfully learning to work with variance. We have all heard stories that say don't buy a new automobile that was assembled on Monday or Friday. Why? Auto defects and complaints about workmanship are associated with the day of the week the car was assembled. Likewise, I recently heard a teacher say that if she were teaching

something that the students really needed to learn and retain, she would teach it on Tuesday through Thursday. Why? Maybe these students aren't as engaged on Mondays or Fridays as they are Tuesday, Wednesday, and Thursday! Examining variance would help us identify and document this problem. In later chapters, several different data tools are available for examining variability as well as central tendency.

Customization of Service

We've come a long way from the days when Henry Ford said, "You can have any color of car you want as long as its black!" Adults in the United States have become accustomed to, maybe even addicted to, the customization of service. We were raised to believe that we are unique and special. We raise our own children to believe that they are unique and special. As a result, we expect to be treated in a unique and special manner. Businesses and industries that compete for our dollars know that they must customize services and products to keep our business.

Schools are now caught in the same syndrome. In most states, public schools no longer enjoy the virtual and protected monopolies they once did. As the schools of choice, school charters, and voucher movements grow, public schools are going to have to compete for students if they want to stay in business. To compete, schools must find ways of meeting customer needs through customization of service. Of course this begins with questions like, *What do parents like and dislike about our school? What do parents care most about when it comes to the education of their children?*

Conducting a needs assessment is an excellent way to uncover this information. Later in this book, you will find a section on how to design and conduct a survey that will help you collect this information from parents and other stakeholders.

This is a radical change for public schools that have historically been held to a standard of "sameness." The courts, communities, and policymakers have long held that all students should be treated the same: same length of school

day, same length of school year, same textbooks. As a matter of fact, when asked what equal educational opportunity means in the classroom, most teachers say, "treat all students the same."

While we have never truly met the goal of treating all children the same, we have come close enough in enough instances to know that…

> Equal treatment will not yield equal results.

It is time to recognize an alternative paradigm. The emerging definition of equal educational opportunity embedded in the accountability movement is that of treating each student in a manner fitting to their needs.

> Clearly, if we want all students to perform at a high level in the curriculum, we must differentiate and customize service.

For many educators, this represents a whole new paradigm of teaching and learning.

My friend and colleague, the late Ron Edmonds, used to say that students know how to learn in more ways than we know how to teach. This is as true today as when he first said it many years ago. The challenge for the school reformer is to help teachers to teach in the many ways students learn. Only then will we truly come close to the vision of "learning for all."

KEY CONCEPTS

- Continuous improvement is a journey and never a destination.

- The continuous improvement cycle recommended here includes the following steps:

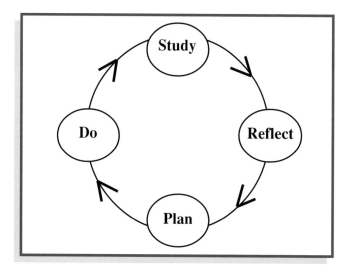

- Continuous school improvement requires customization of services to meet student needs—Equal treatment does not yield equal results.

INTEGRATING THE THEORIES

Each of the three theories—Effective Schools, Systems Theory, and Continuous Improvement Theory—makes a valuable and unique contribution to our discourse on sustainable school reform. As we begin to weave the tapestry of school reform, you will come to see clearly how each compliments the others. You will develop a deeper appreciation for the tools and techniques each theory brings to the reform conversation. Finally, and perhaps most importantly, as you become more familiar with them and what they can offer, you will see new hope for creating sustainable school reform grounded in the mission of "learning for all."

Figure 4.5

Chapter 5

Teams

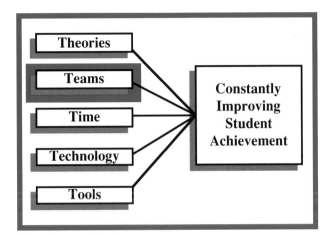

Continuous school improvement is a collaborative process. As such, the school-based team is the cornerstone of its success. This team works to initiate, manage, and facilitate the change process. But why use a team at all? Wouldn't it be more efficient to have the superintendent or principal decide what needs to be changed and direct staff to implement it? Perhaps. But teams provide an opportunity to solicit different perspectives, encourage innovative thought, and foster stakeholder buy-in. After all…

> *None of us is as smart as all of us!*
>
> — Blanchard, et al., 2001

In fact, an effective site-based team and "the synergy gained through cooperation may accomplish for the school what never could be achieved by individuals working independently." (Maeroff, 1993)

Establishing the Site-Based Team as the Engine of Change

Developing an inclusive team that represents the various stakeholders can be a daunting process. After all, individuals bring different attitudes, values, and experiences to the team. They have different perspectives as teacher, parent, administrator, or community member. In addition to the diversity of the team members, team collaborative efforts also may face a variety of barriers.

- **Institutional Disincentives.** These include limited resources to support the team's activities; the existing comfort level with how things are currently done; or a tangled bureaucracy that inhibits efforts for change.

- **Historical and Idealogical Barriers.** Often characterized by long-standing adversarial relationships—union vs. management; perhaps even district vs. school.

- **Power Disparities.** Concerns about preserving institutional power. For example, a district may be hesitant to embrace site-based management and give the school the resources and power to make substantive changes.

- **Differing Perceptions of Risk.** Our various perceptions of risk frame how we view a problem and its potential solutions. Teachers who view the school improvement process as simply an increase in their already overloaded schedule will not readily embrace collaboration.

- **Technical Complexity.** Feeling overwhelmed by the complexity of the task or lacking the needed skills.

- **Political and Institutional Barriers.** The current political press for improved education and the advent of high-stakes testing are pushing schools and school districts to change and change quickly. This can limit the collaborative process because, by its nature, collaboration initially takes more time than top-down implementation programs. However, collaboration usually turns out to be more efficient— and more effective—in the long run.

To overcome these barriers, "we need to switch from an image of individual sovereignty . . . to one of shared stewardship." (Gray, 1989)

Who should be on the Team?

> *Probably the most important criterion for assuring acceptance and successful change is participation.*
>
> — Vogt & Murrell, 1990

A key underlying assumption to the participative process is simply *that the people who will be affected by the plans and decisions made through the improvement process should have a role in making these plans and decisions.* A well-selected team can represent the school structure through which various perspectives flow, and ensure that the school improvement process has a broad base of support. Therefore, the team should reflect a microcosm of the school community. (McCue, 1987)

The chances of achieving success are greater when representatives of key groups are involved. For the most effective group dynamics, team size should be limited to eight to ten participants. However, the politics of a building may influence both composition and size. One way to accommodate both efficiency and openness is to maintain a smaller formal "working" group, but to hold open meetings that are accessible to anyone who is interested. This open meeting format helps to assure that all who have a vested interest are part of the decision-making process.

Each school should develop a procedure for team selection. In some schools, the faculty votes or appoints members to serve. In others, the principal selects from among volunteers. We strongly recommend self-selection or election by a majority of staff, rather than appointment by the principal, faculty council, or parent-teacher association. Generally, an already established work group (e.g., curriculum council, faculty advisory committee, etc.) should not be designated as the school improvement team. The school improvement process is new, and it should not be burdened from the start by having to carry the baggage usually associated with established committees or groups.

The Critical Role of the Principal

The principal is a key player on the school improvement team, providing the leadership to guide the team through the process. However, a principal's leadership style must adapt as the team changes and grows. "Leadership itself keeps on being redefined as community builds. Principals, for example, have to think about leadership one way when they and teachers do not share the same goals and another way when goal consensus begins to emerge." (Seriovanni, 1994) The goal of the principal should be to empower his/her staff. As William Bailey suggests in *School Site Management Applied* (1991), "There is no power equal to sharing the responsibility with other professionals, training them to take responsibility, developing them to be interdependent, and watching people and programs grow."

The principal plays such a crucial role in school improvement that it is wise for individuals in this role to think about their expectations as they approach the school improvement process. If you are a principal, consider the following questions:

- Are you personally ready to take an objective look at practices in your school?

- Are you willing to consider both the strengths and weaknesses of your instructional programs?

- Are you ready to accept criticism and hear frustrations about you or your role as an instructional leader?

- Can you accept and work with people at their level of readiness?

- Are you prepared to provide additional guidance and support to the team as it learns to operate in a new role?

- What priority will you place on the school improvement process in relation to competing projects and demands?

- What is your leadership style? Are you able and willing to adapt that style as the team evolves?

As you embark on this process with a clear idea of your expectations, remember to clear your calendar! Regularly scheduled meetings are important to discuss problems, celebrate small successes, and to coordinate activity. The team needs you. Be there!

Involving Teachers and Staff

Staff who are on the school improvement team become the

ambassadors for the change process to the rest of the faculty and, therefore, are instrumental to the successful implementation of any school improvement efforts. The following suggestions are adapted from the Rhode Island Educational Leadership Academy (1986) and are useful in informing and encouraging staff to become team members:

1. Describe the improvement stages with related processes, both orally and in writing.

2. Describe the tasks and time commitments to staff, both orally and in writing.

3. Extend invitations to participate to all—with opportunity to decline gracefully or to become involved in other ways at the implementation or monitoring stages.

4. Address the personal concerns that people might have about becoming involved. Who supports and finances the effort? Will in-service credit be available? When will meetings be scheduled?

5. Describe the training and support available to help team members get the job done. Determine the need for assistance in conducting meetings, making group decisions, dealing with conflicts, or gathering, analyzing, and interpreting data.

Parents

Some schools elect to have parents represented on the school improvement team at the initiation of the process. Others prefer, at least during the first year, to have the actual working meetings for faculty only while keeping parents aware of all activities and findings. The decision of whether or not to involve parents actively as school team members will be dictated by past practices, community politics, and staff consensus. Whichever way you choose to begin, the long-term goal should be to incorporate parents as full partners in the school improvement process.

Other Participants

Depending on your circumstances, you may want to include individuals from other stakeholder groups, including representatives from the community-at-large, students, the district central office, or noncertified staff. **Remember, involvement increases commitment and commitment is essential to the effective team.**

> *Individual commitment to a group effort—that is what makes a team work, a company work, a society work, a civilization work.*
>
> — Vince Lombardi

Building an Effective Team

Highly effective teams are composed of groups of committed individuals who trust each other; have a clear sense of purpose about their work; are effective communicators within and outside the team; make sure everyone in the team is involved in decisions affecting the group; and follow a process that helps them plan, make decisions, and ensure the quality of their work. (Williams, Byham, & Wilson, 1991)

This description of a highly effective team is consistent with most of the current literature on teams. But effective teams do not occur simply because a group of people have been brought together and told they are on a team. Teams, like continuous school improvement itself, go through stages of development. In 1979, Francis and Young defined these stages as *Testing, Infighting, Getting Organized,* and *Mature Closeness.* A decade later, Williams, Byham, & Wilson defined them *as Getting Started, Going in Circles, Getting on Course,* and *Full Speed Ahead.* Most recently, Ken Blanchard, et al, (1998) identified the four stages as *Orientation, Dissatisfaction, Production,* and *Integration.* Whatever you choose to call them, the four stages of team development are amazingly consistent among researchers.

Team growth is not always a linear process. The circumstances under which the team operates often change; members come and go, new mandates are handed down from the central office or the state, resources are cut, and the like. In response, a team may regress to an earlier stage, at which time the team leader must take the appropriate action to help the team move forward.

Team Training

How easily and quickly a team progresses through these four stages depends, to a great degree, on the process skills of its members. For a team to be effective, its members need a core set of individual skills. These include problem-solving skills, team-building and team-maintenance skills, interpersonal skills, and self-assessment/self-awareness skills. Most people need training in one or more skill areas. The list on page 50 identifies a variety of individual and team process skills that are extremely useful to team members.

We cannot stress enough how important team training is to the success of the process. These basic skills empower team members and cause them to create an empowered and effective team.

Individual and Team Process Skills

I. **Problem-Solving Skills**
    A. Brainstorming
    B. Clarifying
    C. Prioritizing
    D. Checking for consensus
    E. Action planning

II. **Team-Building and Maintenance**
    A. Establishing norms, mission, goals
    B. Building open agendas
    C. Understanding of group process and dynamics

III. **Interpersonal Skills**
    A. Active listening
    B. Giving and accepting positive feedback
    C. Conflict resolution
    D. Risk taking

IV. **Self-Assessment/Self-Awareness Skills**
    A. Stress management
    B. Increased confidence/self-esteem
    C. Leadership skills
    D. Sharpened introspection/self-awareness

Figure 5.1

Focusing the Team

The team has certain responsibilities at each stage of the school improvement process. Those responsibilities rest on a clear understanding of the team's purpose. This purpose must be challenging and compelling, one that "commits and motivates people to work together." (Blanchard & Bowles, 2001) In fact, it is a good idea for the team to formalize their purpose or mission in writing. This document should state "what the team wants to accomplish, why it is important, and how the team will work together to achieve results." (Blanchard & Bowles, 2001) In general, the purpose of the school improvement team will be to facilitate the school improvement process and provide the leadership needed to guide the faculty through the stages in an inclusive and collaborative manner. The following chart outlines team responsibilities and suggested practices:

Team Responsibilities

- Facilitating the discussion of what staff values and helping achieve consensus on the school's purpose.

- Facilitating the development (or review) of the building mission statement.

- Collecting and analyzing student data; sharing the results and facilitating discussions with and among faculty, parents, and other stakeholders.

- Analyzing and sharing results of Correlate assessment.

- Assisting staff in the identification of instructional strengths and concerns.

- Facilitating the setting of school improvement goals.

- Reviewing research and proven practices and sharing information with staff to assist them in determining strategies and activities.

- Designing evaluation procedures.

- Preparing the written improvement plan.

- Monitoring progress on plan implementation.

Figure 5.2

Team Practices

The following suggestions, adapted from *Team Organization* (Erb and Doda, 1989), are designed to provide effective use of team planning time. Teams that pay attention to internal management issues usually find themselves to be more productive than teams that do not. Therefore, teams should:

- Set a regular time and plan to meet.

- Solicit agenda items for the next meeting at the close of each meeting.

- Solicit agenda items between meetings.

- Solicit agenda items from non-team staff as needed.

- Prepare realistic agendas that are balanced in focus (e.g., repetitive

discussions of at-risk students can become counterproductive).

- Set specific goals or target items for each meeting.

- Open one meeting each month with one or two minutes of round robin sharing to address "joys and concerns."

- Keep agendas and meeting minutes in a team file or notebook.

- Post agendas and meeting minutes in the office and/or teachers' lounge.

- Distribute meeting minutes to staff and other stakeholders.

Figure 5.3

Team Failure and Success

> *Most frequent explanation for team failure is a loss of focus on the issue or goal. Ineffective teams are often characterized by goals that are unfocused, politicized, diluted by competing goals, superceded by individuals goals, or a lost sense of urgency.*
>
> — Larson & LaFasto, 1989

Throughout the literature on teams and team building, one overriding theme emerges. Effective and successful teams have one thing in common. They are made up of members who have a clear and mutual understanding of the mission of the team, and are committed to that mission, the organization they serve, and their team.

Those who can meet this challenge are, according to John Brown and Cerylle Moffett, heroes. They believe that heroic educators are "men and women who have been able to overcome their personal, psychological, cultural, and organizational limitations to achieve a higher form of professionalism on behalf of students….To be heroic, either as an individual or as a school organization, is to accept the responsibility and to sustain the commitment (despite both external obstacles and tests of internal fortitude) for confronting and resolving the critical problems that are facing education today. The times demand that we act with courage, vision, integrity, moral purpose, and extraordinary caring for both our colleagues and the children we serve." (1999)

> By the simple act of reading this book and taking the first steps toward school improvement, you are stepping up to the role of "hero."

KEY CONCEPTS

- The school improvement team is the engine of change.

- The team should be diverse and inclusive, representing all relevant stakeholders. Involvement = Commitment

- Effective teams don't just happen—team members need training, time to meet, and recognition of effort and successes.

Chapter 6

Time

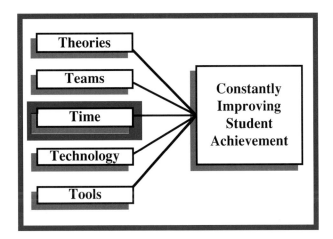

Time is at a premium for all of us, and schools are no different. Given a finite amount of time, finding time to plan and implement change becomes a matter of deciding what is important to us. Often change is resisted because it is perceived as just "one more thing" added to our already packed schedule—another meeting, another initiative, or another activity to cram into an already overfilled day. Therefore, the first requirement for finding time is…

Commitment

Commitment to continuous school improvement by all stakeholders is essential to making the time to plan and implement change. This commitment must begin with the leadership. According to *Finding Time for School Improvement* by the Middle Cities Education Association (MCEA) in Okemos, MI, there must be "a clear commitment to ongoing school improvement by the district leadership, the Board, Superintendent, teacher leaders and building administrators . . . This shared commitment underlies the decision-making process used to allocate limited resources, including time." At the school level, it is the principal's responsibility to see that time is available for planning, training, and implementing change. This communicates the importance of the process, as well as the leadership's commitment to continuous school improvement, to all those involved. The leader must also help everyone involved understand the value of the continuous school improvement process, not only to student outcomes, but to each participant as well.

A common problem of many groups is that they are committed to improvement, but they want it over and done with quickly. So quickly, in fact, that they pounce on the "quick fix." This helps to explain why so many educators believe that the solution to any learning problems in their school requires the purchase of the latest off-the-shelf program. So we highlight the next requirement for finding the time . . .

Understanding

Everyone involved in the process must understand that continuous school improvement is just that...continuous. **It is a process that can begin at any time, but—by definition—can never be finished.** Continuous and sustainable school improvement may best be thought of as an "endless journey." To be successful and sustainable, we can't take a "special event" approach to the process. It has to be integrated into the everyday routine of the classroom, school, and district. Why? Because the sustained success of the reform effort will be in the daily monitoring and adjusting of classroom, school, and district activities to meet the needs of students and the teachers who instruct them. "Whereas, if you achieve a certain level and stop there, and try to hold it there, you run into the law of entropy, leading to certain decline." (Dolan, 1994)

Those involved with the change process must also understand that in order to choose the appropriate strategies for change, they must take the time to define the problem, collect pertinent information, identify and evaluate alternatives, and examine the research and proven practices. To do otherwise—to go for the "quick fix"— is to risk wasting precious time and resources fixing a nonexistent problem or pursuing an ineffective solution.

Finally, we need to understand that time spent in planning, studying, and evaluating—that is, in activities other than teaching—is not "unproductive" time. We are a society of "do-ers" who tend to dismiss the need for study and reflection, both of which are essential to the success of our continuous school improvement efforts. In addressing this attitude, Patrick Dolan, author of *Restructuring Our Schools: A Primer on Systemic Change*, says it well:

Somebody has got to say to the community, to the parents, to the state legislature 'In order to teach your children better...we need to have time to figure out how to do it better, how to improve. We need time to sit down with you, to sit down with each other, with children, to find out what's working and what isn't. . .' Somehow [we] will need to find the courage and commitment to say, 'We will find the time for teachers to spend doing this reflective work . . .' It will take courage because, for the community at large, quality improvement often translates into increasing 'contact days' in the classroom. Somehow the community must be educated to the need for increased time for thinking, planning, communication and problem solving.

Carving Out The Time

Now that everyone agrees that the process will take time and is willing to allocate it, the practical question of where to physically carve out the necessary time must be addressed.

The MCEA surveyed Michigan public school districts asking about their approaches to creating/finding time for school improvement, problems they encountered, and their evaluation of the effectiveness of the approaches they used.

Volunteer Time

Volunteer time is time spent outside of the school day to focus on school improvement issues. For example, teachers may use before and after school, during lunchtime, and weekend or summer breaks for workshops and planning sessions. This may be complemented with "hour-for-hour" or "day-for-day" time whereby donated staff time is matched with equal release time.

It was widely felt by all the responding districts that volunteer time is not sufficient in and of itself because it is inherently limiting. Plus, since staff members are not mandated to be there, there may not be consistent attendance of key members. Another disadvantage of volunteer time is that it is usually scheduled during "downtime" when people are not at their best.

Furthermore, teaching is really the only profession in which we would even consider asking people to volunteer their time outside of work. "You wouldn't go into a steel mill and say . . . 'Could some of you guys please stay over and help us figure out how to make better steel?' You wouldn't do that; the workplace would explode. But for some reason, we expect teachers to do that." (Dolan, 1994)

What other approaches can we take beyond asking teachers to volunteer their time?

Existing Time

Existing time falls into several categories including:

- **Teacher Release.** Schools use many methods to provide teachers release time, including hiring substitutes on either an as-needed basis or a permanent floating basis, using administrators to take classes, or exchanging planning periods with other teachers.

- **Faculty/Department Meetings.** More and more administrators are using these meetings for school improvement and handling the day-to-day operational needs in other ways, such as memos.

- **Combining Classes.** Students can be combined into groups as large as a whole-school assembly to free up most of the faculty, or as small as two classes combined to provide the necessary release time for a single teacher.

- **Schedule Arrangements.** Planning teaching schedules to provide common planning time for teachers involved on the same project.

New Time

New time can be added through a variety of contract arrangements. Some districts arrange early dismissal of school or a delayed start to provide one hour to a half-day of additional time. In one district, junior and senior high teachers were able to gain a weekly three-hour time block for school improvement, staff development, and curriculum planning by adding 30 minutes to the daily calendar. Stipends for staff members involved in school improvement activities beyond contract working hours are another effective way to create new time. Another option is to hire additional full- or part-time staff to coordinate school improvement activities, curriculum planning, or staff development. The use of substitutes is another option, but many teachers are hesitant to embrace this option, since learning often comes to a halt on "sub days" which are generally filled with "busywork." Some schools employ a permanent, rotating substitute teacher who may be better able to maintain the level of learning in the classroom because of the ongoing relationship with the school and its teachers.

There are many creative solutions to finding the time for school improvement. Brainstorming would be an excellent tool to help identify additional methods for finding time. If you and your school are truly committed to the continuous improvement process, you will find a way.

KEY CONCEPTS

Sources of Staff Time for School Improvement

- Volunteer time
- Use of substitutes
- Exchanging planning periods with other staff
- Administrators covering classes
- Use of faculty/departmental meetings
- Combining classes to free up staff
- Coordinating teaching schedules for staff involved in common projects
- Additional paid time added to the school day or week
- Additional paid staff to facilitate school improvement activities

Finding time requires COMMITMENT to the continuous school improvement process. Making time for staff to participate in the process must be a priority at all levels, beginning with the leadership.

Chapter 7

Technology

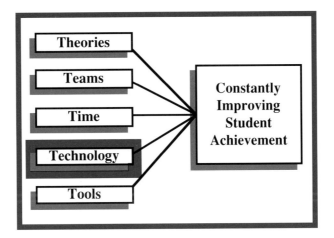

Technology and time, in many ways, are closely linked. On the plus side, technology has the potential to streamline processes and save a significant amount of time for teachers. It can also allow teachers and administrators to make decisions based on facts, not on intuition. Lastly, and perhaps most importantly, it can facilitate student achievement by allowing continuous monitoring and just-in-time intervention for struggling students. However, technology can also be an unwieldy beast, consuming inordinate amounts of time and generating significant amounts of frustration, particularly if it is instituted without clear goals, careful planning, and adequate staff training.

According to Howard Rheingold, author of *The Virtual Community: Homesteading on the Electronic Frontier* and other books about technology, "Computers won't solve the problems of the educational system, [but] ignoring the need to integrate technology into education will exacerbate those problems. We can't afford to do nothing. We can't afford to do the wrong thing. We need to start by thinking about what we *are* doing." We would add that we also need to think about where we want to go . . . that is to begin with the end in mind.

Technology should not simply be an end in and of itself. To use technology to its potential, we have to move beyond making our students "computer literate" and integrate its use into the very fabric of continuous school improvement. Indeed, I would suggest that the ability of technology to provide real time information is key to successful sustainable improvement in student achievement and that without it, it will be far more difficult, if not impossible. That said, simply having educational technology won't necessarily translate into higher student achievement outcomes.

To that end, we must examine our use of technology within the context of sustainable school reform. Let us consider these applications:

- A communication tool

- A learning tool

- A learning assessment tool

- A data collection tool

- An accountability tool

Communication Tool

The advent of the Internet and e-mail has revolutionized our ability to communicate with one another. Schools and school districts can use Web pages to communicate information about themselves to parents and the community. Some schools post their mission and values, a virtual tour of the school, staff biographies, curriculum requirements, special events and activities, the school year calendar, and even the lunch menu. Often teachers have their own Web pages where they post homework assignments and due dates, and links to outside resources that students access from school or home to assist in homework. This can facilitate parent involvement in their child's education by keeping parents aware of current homework assignments, upcoming schedule changes, and special events. The ability for parents to e-mail teachers with questions and concerns can facilitate an ongoing dialog about student progress. The Grand Ledge school district in central Michigan has even instituted a program where parents can check student academic progress in every class at any time. This allows parents to be informed of academic problems long before report cards are issued and provides the opportunity for parents to work with the teacher and student to avoid a failing grade.

Technology has also provided an excellent way for teachers to collaborate, allowing them to share lesson plans and other teaching strategies. The Effective Schools League™, a Web-based program, is one example of using technology as a communication tool for staff. Within a local community of users (a school or a district), the administrator can pose a question or identify an issue, and ask teachers to respond through the "threaded discussion" feature. The administrator could also send e-mails to all community members, announcing upcoming staff development sessions and requesting that individuals r.s.v.p. via e-mail.

A tool such as the League can also link practitioners within or across districts or states. For example, all the special education teachers in a state, the principals within a district, or the superintendents across the nation could use this tool to network and dialog, share questions, views, concerns, and solutions in a time-effective, and therefore cost-effective, way.

Learning and Learning Assessment Tool

Using the computer in the classroom has many benefits for students and teachers alike. Unfortunately, there is a virtual sea of software programs from which to choose. So how can a team choose what software is appropriate to their school? There are several things to keep in mind.

> Good technology with poor content is useless.

Make sure the programs you choose focus on the skills and information you want students to learn.

> Good content with poor technology is almost as bad.

Nothing turns a student off faster than rote drill and practice, whether it's on paper or on a computer. "The best stuff is the stuff that is experiential, exploratory . . . promoting inquiry-based learning," says Evelyn Woldman, technology coordinator at the Massachusetts Elementary School Principals' Association.

Students and teachers alike need feedback on how students are progressing. Teaching technology should incorporate immediate feedback systems so that students and teachers know what students have learned and what they need to review. The use of computerized practice tests, the ability to get immediate results on homework, and the ability to see correct solutions developed on the screen are a few of the available tools for assuring student learning.

Data Collection Tool

At no time in history have we been able to collect the sheer amount and types of data that we can today. While we as a society are "data rich," we are in fact "information poor." That is why it is imperative to have a framework for collecting data, such as the leading indicators of learning discussed earlier in this book. By using the leading indicators to frame our data collection efforts, we collect only meaningful data—data that, when analyzed, can significantly impact student achievement.

For example, if an instructional management system was designed that allowed teachers to frequently monitor student engagement in school, many long-term learning difficulties could be avoided. Such a system could identify students who are not engaged by monitoring absences, suspensions and disciplinary actions, and participation (or lack thereof) in school activities. If the school has a just-in-time intervention system, help can be deployed as soon as a student first shows evidence of disengaging from school and many, many student failures could be prevented.

Accountability Tool

The standards and accountability movement has added significantly to the pressure teachers and schools feel. Some would argue that the level of pressure has become so high as to be unhealthy for many educators caught in the accountability crunch. One strategy that can help educators relieve some of this pressure and still satisfy the demands for accountability would be to use technology to breakdown the tasks into more manageable units. For example, if we have an aligned curriculum, grade-level standards, and formative assessments of those grade-level standards, we could monitor day-to-day whether students are mastering the intended curriculum. The results of assessments used to hold educators accountable should not surprise the teachers who teach the students if student mastery has been monitored all along the way. The formative assessments that teachers use could be delivered by technology. For example, programs like Accelerated Reader™ (produced by Renaissance Learning, Inc.) use student assessments to provide feedback to the student and monitoring information to the teacher.

When the concept of frequent monitoring of student progress is integrated with computers and other technologies, accountability becomes much less intimidating and much more a strategy for helping students to succeed. These applications of available technology will not likely occur unless the school has made a commitment to the notion of giving voice to the data and recognizing the power that comes with just-in-time information.

Navigating the Technology Maze

An excellent guide to thinking about technology is offered by technical writer Steve Bosak. In "All Together Now: A Guide through the Collaborative Technology Jungle," (*electronic school*, January 2000), he offers the following steps:

1. **Don't let technology lead the project.** Decide what you want and how you want to use the technology in teaching, assessment, and communication and then look for the software and hardware that best meet those needs.

2. **Set priorities.** Identify the most important projects and work outward from there.

3. **Decide whether you want dedicated groupware, extranets, or intranets.** Think in terms of growth . . . what technology will allow you to expand into other areas? Bosak suggests that "web-based or Internet-based products will probably remain viable the longest, be easiest to integrate, and give the greatest flexibility in implementing additional groupware strategies."

4. **Consider your budget.** Don't forget to incorporate the costs of upgrades, ongoing maintenance, and staff training. Also, keep in mind the cost of setting up security measures such as firewalls and secure servers.

5. **Begin with pilot projects.** During this stage, involve those who will be most directly involved in the project to help de-bug and enhance the system to ensure that it will meet the school or district's needs.

6. **Roll out in stages.** "Before you open your system to all users, post an outline of major content and application areas with little or no content and ask a representative group of early users for their reactions. . . . At

this point, you'll be testing the navigation of the site, the applications, and the security."

7. **Refine and expand.** Bosak suggests that you poll users regularly and use their comments to enhance, expand, or even delete elements of the design to make it as user-friendly as possible. Then, when one content area is up and running smoothly, you can move to the next priority, keeping in mind how it will logically progress from and interface with the current system.

Clearly, technology can assist us in evaluating our school or district's current position in relation to our goals and to the standards set by the state and the district. It can also identify students in trouble early on and allow us to provide timely and appropriate help. Finally, it can also help us communicate and disseminate vital information to our various stakeholders so that they become involved and supportive of our efforts. Indeed, as expressed by the Jackson, Mississippi Public Schools, "provision of an efficient, effective IMS [instructional monitoring system] requires the use of technology."

Technology Review Form

Figure 7.1

Use the form below to review how you currently use technology and some ideas as to how you could incorporate it into your school.

Technology as a...	Current	Potential
Communication Tool		
Learning Tool		
Assessment Tool		
Data Collection Tool		
Accountability Tool		

KEY CONCEPTS

- Technology and just-in-time information are key components to effective and efficient school reform.

- Within the context of continuous school improvement, technology has several vital applications.

- Technology can help turn data into useful information.

- Technology can help facilitate information sharing and open communication among all stakeholder groups.

Chapter 8

Data-Gathering Tools

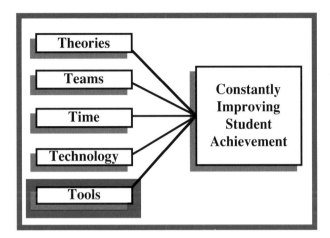

One of the most common data-gathering tools is the survey or needs assessment.

The logic of conducting a survey is obvious and compelling—goals for change should be based on need. Assessing needs in a school means different things to different people. One of the more common needs assessment strategies is to ask individuals, in a position to have an informed opinion, to indicate what they perceive to be the strengths and needs in a school. The information that comes from such a process is valuable if the process used to assess school needs is carefully planned and well executed.

Survey research is a science. It has been used in a variety of very sophisticated and creative ways. The results of surveys have been used to accurately predict elections, project product markets, judge national trends, and shape public policy. The possibilities are virtually limitless. However, survey research has limitations. Carefully collected survey data can give you a clear picture of how different individuals or groups perceive various dimensions of your school. For the most part, the survey data do not tell you why people feel as they do, nor generally give much guidance as to what should be done to solve perceived problems or change perceptions.

Survey Research Guidelines

Conducting a quality survey consists of several interdependent tasks, including developing the questionnaire, selecting the sample, collecting responses from those surveyed, and analyzing and reporting the results. Here are a few suggestions to assist you:

Developing the Questionnaire

How long should our survey be?

On the one hand, the questionnaire should be long enough, and include enough items, so that the results form a comprehensive and accurate picture of the school. On the other hand, the longer the questionnaire, the less likely it is that some respondents will take the time to complete it. Keep the questionnaire as short as possible while still covering the subject. Design it so that it can be carefully and comfortably completed in 30 minutes or less.

Most survey questions use a five-point Likert Scale (e.g., Strongly Agree to Strongly Disagree). This format allows the school team to include more items and minimizes the time it takes respondents to complete the survey. If the respondents are expected to write out their answers, obviously more time will be required to complete the questionnaire and fewer items can be included.

When you write the instructions to the questionnaire, be sure to indicate, as clearly as possible, why you are conducting the survey, how important the responses are, and your best estimate of how long it will take to complete the survey.

Make sure the items you include on your survey are simple and straightforward. A common problem encountered by inexperienced survey writers is to ask two questions in one (for example, "The students in our

school are highly motivated to learn and are respectful of teachers." As a respondent, I may strongly agree that students are highly motivated, but disagree that students are respectful of teachers. How should I respond to the "strongly agree to strongly disagree" scale? This item must be separated into two questions.

Is there a way to keep the respondent from thoughtlessly giving the same answer to every question?

Survey researchers are always concerned about "response set." When the respondent finds that his/her answer to the first 10 questions is "strongly agree," he/she may be tempted to respond the same way to all the questions without even reading them. Survey research specialists have a variety of strategies you can use to reduce the problem of response set. One of the easiest techniques is to word some questions in the positive and some in the negative. Question one might read, "Students in our school are highly motivated to learn." Question two might read, "Students in our school do not respect teachers."

The challenge of reversing some of the items to avoid the problem of response set comes with the analysis and reporting phase of the work. The survey analyst must remember to reverse the scale when reporting the survey results. For example, if respondents strongly disagree to the item that says that students do not respect teachers, that is actually a positive and favorable response.

Once a near final draft of the questionnaire has been prepared, one or two people unfamiliar with it should be invited to respond. If at all possible, choose "testers" who are closely matched to your potential respondents. This pilot effort will allow the team to determine how much time is required to complete it and will pinpoint any problems the respondent may encounter with unclear or confusing items.

Selecting the Sample and Collecting Responses

Ordinarily, survey research is used to develop an accurate picture of how a large group feels about some issue. Time and resource limitations often make it impossible for the survey researcher to collect data from everyone in the population, so sampling is needed. The science of survey research has become very sophisticated in selecting samples that are representative of the population from which they are drawn. It is possible to develop very accurate profiles of the population based on extremely small samples. Fortunately, needs assessment surveys at the school level will not require most of those sophisticated processes.

How large should our sample be?

The guidelines regarding sample size represent a balance between the science of survey sampling and the practical politics of the situation. Carefully selected small samples can give a very accurate picture of the whole group. However, if you want broad commitment and support for the resulting conclusions and

recommendations, you may want to give everyone an opportunity to respond to the survey.

There is no good reason to select a sample of teachers from the total population in your school. It makes more sense to provide every teacher, staff person, and administrator with the opportunity to participate in the survey; you will find that the additional time required to analyze data from the larger group is worth it. Once the survey is administered, you may want to analyze the data for teachers separate from that of other staff.

When it comes to collecting data from parents or students, the total group may be too large to include everyone. In such cases, you may want to select a representative sample from the total group. The ability to generalize from a sample to a total population means that everyone in the population must have an equal chance to be selected in the sample. This is called random sampling. For example, if you are surveying students' attitudes toward the high school and you limit the sample to seniors, the ability to generalize the findings to all students is also limited. You may end up with a very accurate picture of how the seniors feel, but you won't be able to say with certainty that the results represent all the high school students. Because seniors are older and are facing different issues and challenges, they very well may have different opinions than the rest of the student body. Your survey results of seniors, then, are not **generalizable** to the entire student population.

One of the easiest ways to select a sample is to stratify the population according to some characteristic (age, grade, income, school) and select random samples from each stratum. In the case of students, the stratum of most interest might be grade level (e.g., freshman, sophomores, juniors, and seniors). The next step would be to select a fixed percentage of each stratum (e.g., 20 percent).

Should the survey be anonymous?

Our recommendations on the question of anonymity try to balance a couple of difficult issues. Certainly, it would be nice to be able to know exactly how each person responded. This would require the respondent's name to be linked directly with his responses. Obviously, there would be no anonymity in this situation. The problem is that many potential respondents will not complete the survey without assurances of anonymity. If you take steps to make sure the respondent's data are anonymous, you can increase the response rate, but you won't know who didn't respond, limiting your follow up.

So what is the best course of action? Always assure anonymity and work through the problems that decision creates. If you promise anonymity, you must take every precaution to make good on your promise. Anyone who may handle the returned questionnaires must be instructed to ignore any identifying information (e.g., a return address on envelope).

Always plan to conduct at least one follow-up reminder to be sure that you get as high a response rate as possible. Since you will not know who has and has not returned the questionnaire, you should plan to send the reminder to everyone with a note that thanks those who have already responded.

A related issue is that of confidentiality. If people give you solicited or unsolicited written comments, you may wish to use them in your final report. If you do, be sure to disguise them as much as possible to avoid tracing the response to a particular individual, grade level, or part of the community.

What response rate do we need for valid data?

When conducting a survey, you hope to get 100 percent of the respondents to return their questionnaires, but that's not likely to happen. Then the question of minimum response rate arises. Obviously, the closer you can come to the goal of 100 percent, the better. A low response rate tends to be of more concern when the size of the survey population is small in the first place. For example, there is more to be concerned about if five teachers out of a survey population of 20 fail to respond than if 50 parents out of 200 don't respond. The reason is that a single teacher's response constitutes five percent of all the respondents, whereas one parent's response constitutes only half of one percent of all the respondents. Because response rate is key to the validity—and credibility—of the results, always report the response rate when presenting the results.

Analyzing and Reporting Survey Data

Assuming that a high quality questionnaire has been carefully prepared and administered to the target group, and an adequate percentage has returned the questionnaire, we now turn to the analysis and reporting of findings. As with all other aspects of survey research, the analysis and reporting phase can range from simple and straightforward to complex with sophisticated statistical testing. In general, it's best to keep the analysis simple and the report straightforward.

What should we consider in analyzing the data from a survey?

Assume the audience will want to know the who, what, where, when, and how associated with the development and administration of the survey. People want the context for the information they are attempting to process. The results should be communicated as simply as possible without distorting the information. Simple distributions with the number and percent of respondents to each category on the Likert Scale associated with each survey item are basic. You may want to draw a graph of the response profile to add visual impact to the report.

The audience is most interested in the meaning you attach to the data. Be careful here. A common error in reporting the findings is to go beyond

the data and infer causation or to rush to judgment about what should be done to solve the perceived problem. However, survey data typically does not allow inferences of causality. The team preparing the report will have an opportunity to draw conclusions and formulate recommendations. This section of the report should be clearly labeled "conclusions and recommendations."

Who should see the report?

It is always a good idea to have the draft of the report read critically by a few people before going to press. The readers can help identify where too little detail was given or something was left out. Likewise, the readers can help to identify those places where the critics might argue that the authors have gone beyond the data or perhaps even misinterpreted it.

Every effort should be made to make the report available to all survey respondents. If the survey population is large and the final report is lengthy, you may want to send out an "Executive Summary" to all respondents and stakeholders, inviting anyone interested to request a copy of the complete report. In addition, all meetings for discussing the findings and conclusions should be open and announced well in advance. Our experience suggests that any action by the team that may be interpreted as closing the circle of communication will increase the level of distrust and cast suspicion on the report.

Interviewing

When faced with gathering data, the school improvement team often wonders what is the best way to collect information. Should we do face-to-face interviews, telephone surveys, or self-administered (paper and pencil or online) surveys? Are there any advantages of one over the other in terms of validity of the data? According to *Improving Interview Method and Questionnaire Design* (Bradburn, et al., 1979), "no one method is clearly superior to all others. Different methods may be appropriate for different studies. The selection of the method of administration will be properly influenced more by other considerations, such as cost, access to the desired sample, and ease of administration, than by the superiority of a particular method in terms of getting more valid data."

Survey Collection Methods

	Written Surveys	Phone Interviews	Face-to-Face Interviews
Advantages	• Inexpensive • Easy to distribute • Higher perceived anonymity	• Higher response rate • Relatively easy • Tracks who did and did not respond	• Most complete information • Highest response rate • Best at reaching high poverty, low literacy respondents
Disadvantages	• Lower response rate • Inability to know who did or did not respond • Limits direct follow-up	• More expensive • Requires accurate record-keeping • Eliminates individuals without a phone from sample • Lower perceived anonymity	• Time consuming • Expensive • Possible interviewer effects • High perceived lack of anonymity

Figure 8.1

That said, there are advantages and disadvantages to each, depending on your situation. Furthermore, your situation may require you to use more than one method of inquiry. You may want to start out with a self-administered survey. The advantage of this is that it is relatively cheap and easy to distribute to your stakeholders, and anonymity is perceived to be higher by the respondents who, in turn, may be more honest and forthcoming in their answers. However, response rate may be small, and you won't know who did not respond.

Telephone interviews will give you a higher response rate and they are relatively easy to do. However, a large sample will require several individuals to do the calling. Excellent record keeping on contacts and call-backs is essential to prevent respondents from being called more than once. Also, respondents may not be as forthcoming because of a perceived lack of anonymity. In very poor areas, you may be eliminating those who cannot afford a phone from your sample.

Face-to-face interviews provide the most complete information, but they are time consuming and expensive to do. There may be some hesitancy on the part of the respondent to be forthcoming because of a lack of anonymity. Proper training of the interviewer is essential in both face-to-face and telephone surveys to minimize the influence of the interviewer on the respondent's answers.

Most school and school districts will do well to use a balanced approach, using written or online questionnaires and then following up with telephone or face-to-face interviews or focus groups to "give voice to the data."

Incorporating Technology into the Survey Process

Schools are increasingly equipped with computers and Internet access. In addition, many American households now have online access as well. This technology has made it even easier to conduct survey research.

The advantages of online surveys include anonymity, speed, and ease of response. Parents, staff, and community members can respond whenever it is convenient, wherever they can access the Internet. For individuals who don't have access to the Internet at home or at work, you can set up survey "stations" at school activities and events like Curriculum Night and encourage stakeholders to take the survey then and there.

There are a variety of Web-based survey tools available. When evaluating this kind of service, you may want to ask about the following features:

• Are surveys easy to create?

• Are the resulting online surveys clean looking, easy to understand and easy to respond to for the user?

• Does the survey tool allow you to write instructions or explanations to help respondents take the survey?

- Can the online survey be formatted and printed in hard copy for distribution as a paper and pencil survey or for reference at committee meetings and in reports?

- Does the tool automatically tally online responses or do you have to hand-enter data?

- Are the data collected compatible with typical spreadsheet technology so that you can disaggregate the data for analysis?

One such tool currently available is Reality Check™, an online survey service that meets the criteria listed above, plus offers a database of over 2,000 questions built around the Correlates of Effective Schools. More information on Reality Check™ is available in the appendix of this book.

Collaborative Data-Gathering Tools

The Role of the Facilitator

The facilitator is an individual who can guide the team or group through the process of using one or more of the data-gathering tools. The facilitator may begin the process by outlining the problem or issue the group is considering and identifying the goal or desired outcome of the process: to identify the cause of a particular problem, generate a list of solutions, etc. The facilitator then instructs the group in how the tool or process works and sets forth the ground rules for participation. From this point on, the facilitator's role is to keep the process

moving and encourage all group members to participate. Occasionally, the facilitator may need to assist the group in mediating conflict or ask probing or clarifying questions to help the group when they become "stuck." Finally, the facilitator may need to steer the group back "on task" if they substantially digress from the process/ goal at hand.

The Role of the Participant

As a participant in one or more of the processes outlined below, we need to make a commitment to the process and to the group. We have to bring an open mind to the table, as well as a willingness to participate and contribute to the discussion in a positive manner. We need to be willing to examine our own "mental models" and to suspend our own assumptions as we dialog with other participants. And we must recognize the inherent value of all participants, and respect their opinions even when we don't agree. Finally, we must accept that conflict is an inevitable—and creative—part of the process and embrace it constructively.

Brainstorming

There are three reasons to use brainstorming: to determine possible causes and/or solutions to problems; to plan out the steps of a project; or to decide which problem (or opportunity) to work on. (Chang & Dalziel, 1999) Brainstorming is also a great way to build consensus. In addition, the process of brainstorming is fundamental to many of the other data-gathering tools.

The idea in brainstorming is to generate as many ideas as possible within the allotted time. No criticism or editing of ideas is allowed. In fact, the wilder and more creative the ideas, the better. This is a tool that is designed to promote "thinking out of the box," and to generate new and innovative approaches to problem solving by building and expanding on each other's ideas. This is commonly referred to as **synergy**: the sum of the whole is greater than its parts.

There are two ways to solicit ideas from group members. One is called **freewheeling**; there is no specific order to generating ideas; individuals shout out ideas as they occur to them. This can be a very high-energy process, and generate a high level of enthusiasm and interaction. However, this format may be somewhat intimidating for the more timid members of the group and discourage them from contributing.

An alternative method is the **round robin**. In this method, the facilitator solicits ideas person-by-person, asking each individual for one idea and going around the circle until everyone is out of ideas. This encourages broad participation and may prevent one or more individuals from dominating the process.

The facilitator may wish to mix methods, beginning with round robin and switching to freewheeling. This is a useful way to reenergize a group that is running out of ideas too quickly.

Asynchronous, Web-based Brainstorming

There are times when you may want to include a much larger group in the brainstorming process or you are unable to get your group together for the brainstorming exercise. One way to achieve similar results is asynchronous, web-based brainstorming.

If the classrooms in your school are linked by computer, you can use your school's intranet program (an Internet-like program within your school) to post the problem on the net and ask for staff to post ideas. An example of this type of program is the Effective Schools League™. As part of your private school community, you can conduct this brainstorming exercise through the threaded discussion feature. As ideas are posted, staff can return to the site as they have time to build on others' suggestions.

Affinity Diagram

Once you've brainstormed a slew of ideas, you'll need a way to organize them. The Affinity Diagram is just the tool you need. "This tool gathers large amounts of language data (ideas, opinions, issues, etc.) and organizes it into groupings based on the natural relationship between each item. It is largely a creative rather than a logical process." (Brassard, 1989)

The affinity diagram is used to "add structure to a large or complicated issue; break down a complicated issue into easy-to-understand categories; gain agreement on an issue or situation." (Chang & Dalziel, 1993) It is especially useful when the group is "stuck" and can't seem to generate new ideas. "When the only solutions are old solutions, try an Affinity to expand the team's thinking." (Chang & Dalziel, 1993)

Steps in Using the Affinity Diagram

- Define the issue, goal, question, objective, problem.

- Use brainstorming to generate ideas.

- Record all ideas on sticky notes or index cards.

- Arrange cards into related groupings.

- Do not force "loners"—cards without a logical group—to fit into other categories. It's okay for a category to have only one card.

- Have everyone move the cards around to the grouping where they think they should be. By making this a silent process, you "encourage unconventional thinking (which is good) while it also discourages semantic battles that can rage on and on (which is bad)." (Brassard, 1989)

- Team members should do this quickly without a great deal of reflection.

- Teams should be encouraged to think "out of the box"—not depend on standard, "safe" categories, but to "allow new groupings to emerge from the chaos of the cards." (Brassard, 1989)

- Create Header Cards: concise (1-5 words); clear (would someone outside your group understand what the heading meant without additional explanation or detail?) Identify the central concept; reflect the "spirit" as well as the content. Some groupings are related and need a "super-header."

- Draw the final diagram for circulation and comments.

Figure 8.2

Creating the Affinity Diagram

1. **Frame the question.**

2. **Brainstorm ideas (round-robin or freewheeling).**

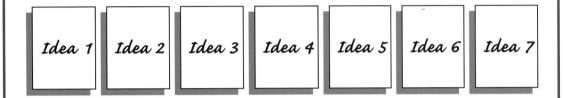

3. **Team members silently arrange cards into logical groupings.**

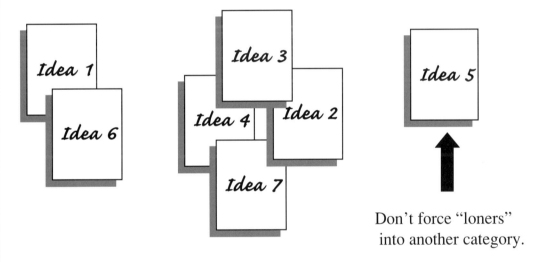

Don't force "loners" into another category.

4. **Create "headers" for groups.**

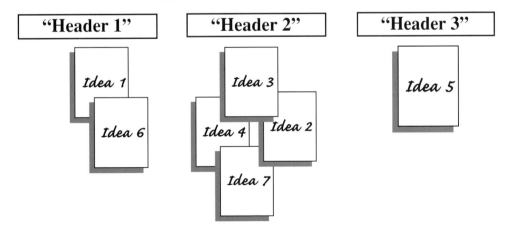

5. **Draw the final diagram and circulate for comments.**

Figure 8.3

Force Field Analysis

Change is a dynamic process, with forces working in your favor (driving forces) and forces working against you (resistance). This tool helps your team to identify those forces.

The team must first agree on the current situation, issue, or problem and then clarify your goal. For example, let's say that your team has decided that adopting a year-round calendar is a needed step toward improved student achievement. The next step is to identify those forces—actions, skills, equipment, procedures, culture, people, resources, etc.—that profoundly affect your goal either positively or negatively. Using our example, you may find that the objections of some parents and a lack of air conditioning during the hot weather are forces against the adoption of a year-round calendar. Conversely, you may identify available grant monies and a supportive central office as forces in favor. The next step is to prioritize the driving and restraining forces. You may sort the driving and restraining forces based on common themes using the affinity diagram.

1. **Identify situation, issue, goal.**

2. **Brainstorm driving/resisting forces.**
    - **actions**
    - **resources**
    - **skills**   **adequate, inadequate, nonexistent**
    - **procedures**
    - **attitudes**
    - **culture**   **positive, negative**

Force Field Analysis

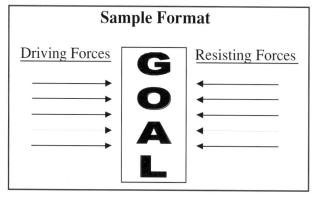

Sample Format

Driving Forces   **GOAL**   Resisting Forces

3. **Prioritize forces.**

4. **Explore reasons behind these forces. Why?**

5. **Develop strategies to weaken resisting forces and strengthen driving forces.**

Figure 8.4

As you identify the resisting and driving forces, you will want to dig deeper and find out why these forces exist. Why do some parents oppose the year-round calendar? Why is the central office so supportive? Once you've identified the reasons behind the forces at work, you can work to lessen the restraining forces and strengthen the driving forces.

Root Causes ("Five Whys" + Data)

A key idea in systems thinking is that the causes of a problem are often not obvious. Without knowing the actual cause of a problem, we can mistakenly adopt the wrong "fix" and, in fact, make the problem worse or simply move the problem to another part of the system.

The Five Whys (Ross, 2001) is a great method for determining the root causes for recurring problems. You begin with your team by choosing a problem or symptom that you are trying to resolve. For example, let's say you want to address the poor performance of a particular group of students on a standardized test. The first question you ask is "Why did these particular students do poorly on the test?" The group then brainstorms reasons for the poor performance. There will probably be several answers. Post them all on a flip chart or chalkboard.

Let's assume that someone suggests that the poor performers do not read well. We can check the accuracy of this by looking at other sources of student achievement data.

Once we've verified that, as a whole, this group doesn't read well, we ask "why" again. "Why don't these students read well?" Again, the group brainstorms possible reasons and again we check the data to verify if our assumptions are borne out. Let's imagine that someone suggests that many students in this group read poorly because their attendance at school is poor. We then check the attendance records of these students and, for purposes of our example, find that these students indeed have poor attendance records. Again, we ask "why?" By the end of the fifth "why," we should have a pretty good idea of the root causes of our students' poor test performance. Then we can focus our energies on finding solutions that will have a better chance of success.

Criteria Rating Form

The Criteria Rating Form is also known as a prioritization matrix and is used to select among several options or solutions. This tool is especially useful when you want to make a decision objectively and eliminate as much personal bias as possible (especially when one or two people come to the table with a "pet" solution). This tool will help you to create consensus or group "buy-in" for a decision as well.

The first step is to list the alternatives and agree on decision criteria. You may use brainstorming to generate the criteria. Give each criterion a weight that reflects its importance relative to the other criteria. The total of all weights must equal 100 percent. You may do this by asking each person to assign weights individually and then average them together to get a group weighting. Then rate each option on a scale of one to ten, with 10 being high and one being low. This may have to be done at a different meeting so that some research may be done to provide solid data on which to base decisions instead of team members' "gut feelings."

Criteria Rating Form

| | Weight | ALTERNATIVES | | | | | |
| | | Alternative A | | Alternative B | | Alternative C | |
		Raw Score	Weighted Score	Raw Score	Weighted Score	Raw Score	Weighted Score
Criteria 1		(1=lowest; 10=highest)	(Weight x Raw Score)				
Criteria 2							
Criteria 3							
Totals	(Must equal 100%)						

Steps for using the Criteria Rating Form

1. Determine decision criteria.

2. Assign each criterian a weight. The sum of all weights must equal 100%.

3. Rate alternatives on a scale of 1 to 10 in relation to each criterion.

4. Multiply the criterion weight by the raw score to get the weighted score.

5. Add all the weighted criterion scores for each alternative. The highest score will be your best alternative based on the relevant criteria.

Figure 8.5

KEY CONCEPTS

- Surveys are designed to collect perceptual data from your stakeholder.

- The steps in survey research include developing the questionnaire, selecting the sample, distributing the questionnaire, collecting the responses, and analyzing and reporting the results.

- Collaborative Data Tools include:

  - Brainstorming
  - Affinity Diagram
  - Force Field Analysis
  - Root Cause Analysis or the Five Whys
  - Criteria Rating Form

- When using collaborative data tools, team members must approach the process with an open mind, a willingness to participate, and respect for other's opinions. After all, **none of us is as smart as all of us!**

Chapter 9

Data-Analysis Tools

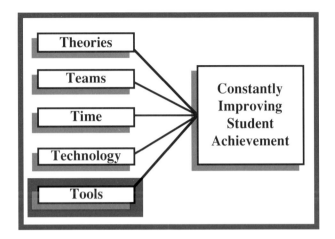

Now that you've collected your data, the next step is to analyze your information.

Statistical analysis can be daunting to those who have had little or no experience with it. However, statistics are merely tools to help you "give voice to the data." Data itself—student scores, numbers of disciplinary problems, etc.—are simply numbers. They tell you very little in their raw form. Statistics allow you to take the data and look at it from different perspectives to get a clearer picture of your situation. The nature of the data dictates what tools you choose for analysis.

Measures of Central Tendency

"The central axis for any mass of data is called the point of central tendency. . . . In statistical language, we call the techniques for finding such a point the measures of central tendency."

(Leedy, 1985) They typically include the mode, the median, and the mean.

Mode

The mode is the most usual score, i.e., whichever score occurs most frequently. For example, out of 100 student test scores, more students score a 78 than any other single score. Seventy-eight is the mode of these 100 scores. When a distribution has a single peak or a single mode, the distribution is considered to be **unimodal**. When a distribution has two peaks or two modes at different parts of the scale, it is said to be **bimodal**.

When a distribution is unimodal with lots of average scores and only a few high and low scores on each side, the resulting graph is bell-shaped. Because this type of distribution is very common, it is often called a normal distribution, the bell curve, or the normal curve.

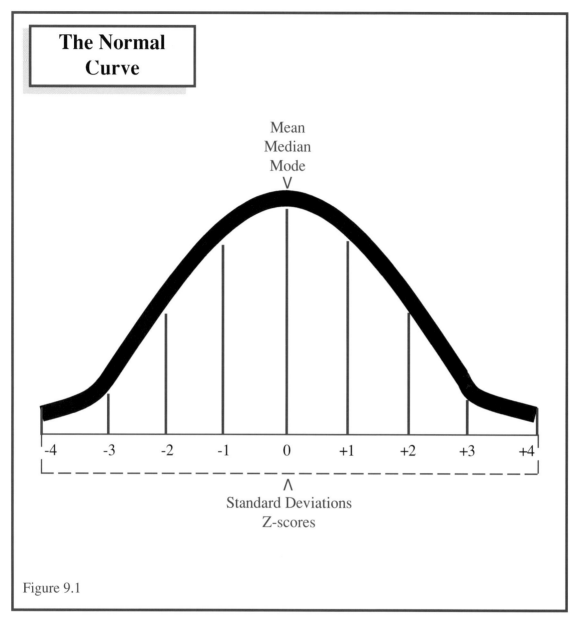

Figure 9.1

The normal curve represents the general distribution that occurs among most characteristics or phenomena in nature. For example, let's consider the human physical characteristic of height. Within a given group of people, you would find that the height of most people would cluster around the middle third of the distribution. A few people would be very short and a few would be very tall. The same would occur whether you were looking at weight or shoe size.

The frequency with which this distribution occurs in nature has caused us to believe—erroneously—that all phenomena must fit the normal curve. When applied to education, it belies a philosophy at odds with the Effective Schools belief that all children can master essential learnings. In fact, the traditional bell-shaped curve shows gradations of student achievement—including failure— as normal and acceptable.

Skewedness

The "normal" distribution can actually take many forms. It can have a high peaked curve that occurs when most of the data cluster around the middle. This would indicate a high level of homogeneity among the data. The normal curve can also have a flattened distribution, with more high and low scores. This would indicate a high level of heterogeneity among the data.

Sometimes the bell curve becomes *skewed*. This means that there are many more scores on one side of the scale. If there are many more low scores than average or high scores, we say the curve is *positively skewed*. If there are many more high scores than average or low scores, we say the curve is *negatively skewed*. The skewedness of test results can indicate that there are characteristics of the test that affected the results. For example, a bell curve of a standardized test that clusters at the low end (is positively skewed) may indicate a lack of alignment between the curriculum and the test, i.e., the students were tested on material that they were never taught. Or the skew could have resulted from the test having a variety of very easy questions that nearly everyone could answer correctly

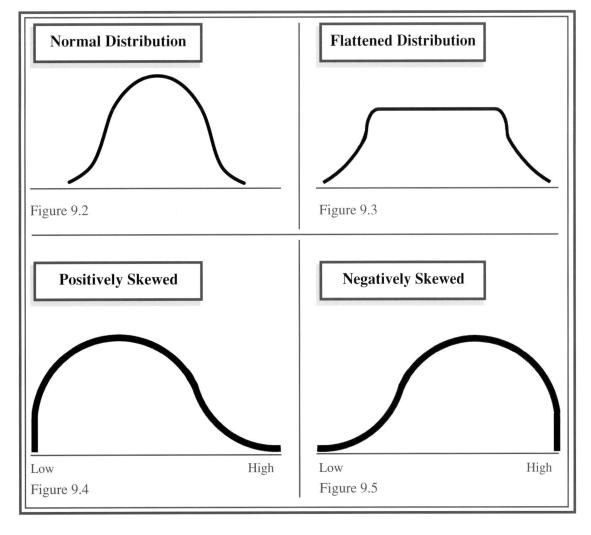

Normal Distribution

Figure 9.2

Flattened Distribution

Figure 9.3

Positively Skewed

Low   High

Figure 9.4

Negatively Skewed

Low   High

Figure 9.5

which eliminated the very low end of the curve. This is called a "floor effect." There are ceiling effects as well, which are evidenced by a negatively skewed bell curve. Ceiling effects result when there aren't enough challenging questions that allow the most able students to excel, eliminating the upper end of the bell curve. However, according to *How to Analyze Data* by Fitz-Gibbon and Morris (1987), "if the test has been designed to measure mastery of certain skills and you expect most of a group [of] students to achieve mastery, then a negatively skewed distribution is what you will want to see."

The J-Curve

A J-curve models a different educational philosophy. The philosophy represented by the J-curve states that virtually all learners can master what is being taught. Some students may need more time and assistance, since we all learn at different rates and in different ways. The J-curve speaks to the need for customization of learning . . . a basic tenet of total quality/continuous improvement theory.

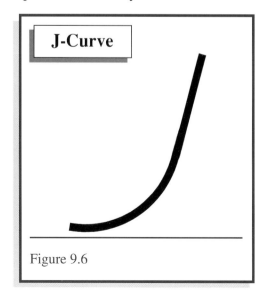

J-Curve

Figure 9.6

Median

The median is the exact numerical center of a data spread. For example, if your data include 10 test scores, the median grade is the one in the middle of the series—50 percent of the scores will be above it and 50 percent below it.

Mean

The mean is the average of a set of scores. It is often referred to as the "balance point." Envision a scale with the scores as weights. The mean would be the point at which the distribution of the scores are balanced evenly on the scale.

The mean is calculated by adding all the scores together and dividing by the number of scores. The mean is used when you want to represent a set of scores with one number. The use of the mean is very popular and can be a useful way of representing group performance. "In the broad setting of possibilities, we are betting on the average as being the best guess as to what is most characteristic." (Leedy, 1985) That said, **you must be cautious when using the mean because it can be very misleading**. The mean is most representative of a group when scores are closely clustered and unimodal. However, the mean can easily be skewed by extreme scores (also called "outliers"), or by scores that are bimodal—having two modes or highest points. The mean would then give the reader a much less accurate picture of how the group as a whole scored on the test.

As you can see, measures of central tendency, by themselves, can give you an incomplete picture of reality. To clarify our picture, we turn to another type of statistic—measures of variability.

Measures of Dispersion and Variability

Measures of variability can show us how the data spread out on either side of the central point.

Range

The range is simply the total spread of the data. For example, the range of a list of scores from 82 to 97 is 15 points. Again, the range is simply descriptive of how far the scores—including the extreme scores—are dispersed. The range must be used in conjunction with the measures of central tendency to give a more accurate picture of the data.

Quartile Range

This refers to the division of the data spread into four equal parts. The first quartile will be the point where 25 percent of the data items fall below. The second quartile is the exact halfway point of the data and is synonymous with the median. The third quartile is the point at which 75 percent of the data items fall below. The quartile range is a way to measure skewedness and is used when the median is selected as the measure of central tendency. The **interquartile range** refers to the data that fall between the first and third quartiles (between the 25th percentage point and the 75th percentage point).

Standard Deviation

Standard deviation is related to the mean (average) of a group of scores. It tells you how much the scores are spread around the mean. The larger the standard deviation, the more spread out the scores are around the mean. In a normal distribution (the bell curve) 68 percent of all scores fall within one standard deviation of the mean.

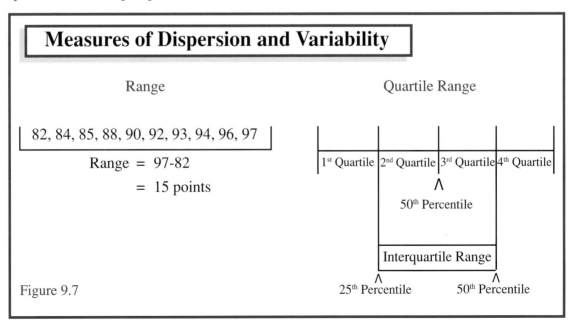

Measures of Dispersion and Variability

Range

82, 84, 85, 88, 90, 92, 93, 94, 96, 97

Range = 97-82

= 15 points

Quartile Range

1st Quartile 2nd Quartile 3rd Quartile 4th Quartile

∧
50th Percentile

Interquartile Range

∧   ∧
25th Percentile   50th Percentile

Figure 9.7

Common Data Transformations

Percentiles

If you convert a set of scores into percentages and then rank order them from 1 to 100, you have created a percentile ranking. A percentile is a point on that scale at or below which a given percentage of the scores fall. For example, if a student scores at the 73rd percentile, he or she can be said to have scored as well or better than 73 percent of the group we are using as a comparison or "norm." Norm-referenced tests like the Stanford Achievement Test (SAT) report student scores as percentiles. According to Deborah Wahlstrom in *Using Data to Improve Student Achievement*, "percentile scores don't tell you how well a student did in relation to specific learning targets or standards, they only tell you what percentage of students were outperformed. Percentile scores range for 1-99, and these scores are not equal interval scores—which means that the distance from 1-10 is not the same as the distance between 40 and 50….A student's percentile rank or group can change from test to test depending on which norming group is used to determine the ranking."

Z-Scores

Z-scores are the distance of an individual score from the mean expressed in standard deviation units. Z-scores always have a value of zero at the mean point. The farther a score falls from the mean, the larger its z-score. Z-scores that fall above the mean carry a plus sign; z-scores that fall below the mean carry a negative sign.

Disaggregating the Data

Descriptive statistics provide tools that allow educators to look for trends, relationships, and instructional effects so they can determine what instructional practices are working. But as discussed above, statistical tools such as the mean can give you an inaccurate picture of how your school is progressing on the "learning for all" mission. Unfortunately, the inaccurate picture is usually more optimistic than reality and often fails to identify significant problems and specific populations that are struggling.

How do we avoid this problem? We must go back to the twin issues of educational quality and educational equity. The research literature has insisted that schools must address these issues by asking—and answering—two questions concerning a school's effectiveness: "Effective at what?" (quality), and "Effective for whom?" (equity). The first of these two questions is answered in terms of student mastery of the essential learnings. This implies that we have defined what we want students to know and be able to do, and that care has been taken to assure that all curricula and assessments are well aligned with the learning objectives. And when students achieve at high levels, that is evidence of this quality.

The second question—"Effective for whom?"—will be answered through the analysis and display of the outcomes data. In the past, most schools have analyzed assessment data based on the aggregate or total population of students. Aggregated measures of achievement are inadequate because they tend to disguise too much of what is really happening in the school. To overcome this problem, the Effective Schools Research suggests that student outcome data be **disaggregated**, or broken down into the major subpopulations present in the school.

For example, let's assume that 57 percent of Oak Middle School's 500 students scored at a proficient level on the state standardized reading test. The faculty's first reaction may be to implement a school-wide reading improvement program. But does the aggregate score tell the whole story? After disaggregating the data by SES, the faculty might find that 80 percent of the middle- and upper-SES students attained proficiency on the reading test, but only 32 percent of low-SES students (which make up nearly half the student population) attained proficiency. This new information puts Oak Middle School's reading scores in a whole new light.

Disaggregation is not a problem-solving strategy; it is a problem-*finding* strategy. It is key to our continuous school improvement model—indeed to every credible problem-solving model—because it's effectiveness depends upon a clear description of the problem. In my experience, school faculties who have conducted a disaggregated analysis find that this step, more than any other, helped them identify their school's problems.

Disaggregating the Right Variables

Just as it is possible to use a limitless variety of different measurements as

evidence of student learning, there are no limits to the subpopulations that could be analyzed. As a rule, it is better to disaggregate outcome data for few rather than many subpopulations. But how do you decide what demographic variables to focus on and be confident that you have selected the appropriate ones?

The educational research literature suggests that certain demographic variables tend to be associated with student achievement. They are gender, race/ethnicity, and socioeconomic status.

Gender, Race/Ethnicity, and Socioeconomic Status (SES)

Research has consistently found gender disparities in both participation and achievement in math and science. Female students at about 8th grade start to fall behind in these areas and the gap continues to grow throughout high school. Much of this disparity is attributed to how girls are engaged and encouraged in the classroom to embrace these academic areas. What would the outcome data look like at your school if the girls as a group were compared with boys as a group? A disaggregated analysis based on gender should show that girls and boys are achieving at similar levels. Alternately, an identified gender gap should serve as the focus for school improvement plans.

The second variable that is often used for disaggregation is that of race and ethnicity. This analysis is not appropriate in some schools because there are too few students in a single ethnic or racial group to yield reliable and meaningful results. (This would be true in a school that was primarily white with very few African-American students or in a primarily African-American school with very few white students.) A good rule of thumb is to only disaggregate data for subgroups that make up 15 percent or more of the total student population. If you have several minority subgroups (Hispanic, African-American, Arab, and Asian) that each make up a small percentage of the total population, it may be appropriate to combine them to form a single larger group for disaggregation. As with the disaggregation of student outcome data based on gender, do not lose sight of the reason for analyzing the data in this way—to determine if your minority and nonminority students are experiencing equal success and if not, why not.

Socioeconomic status (SES) is a major factor in predicting student achievement in many schools. As a matter of fact, SES tends to be a more significant factor than either race or gender. Therefore, we need to determine how well the poor and disadvantaged students, as a group, do in relation to our more advantaged middle- and upper-class students.

In conducting a disaggregated analysis of student outcome data based on SES, a valid and acceptable indicator of SES is needed. The preferred indicator would be parents' education level. If the school can secure this information from the parents, it will prove to be relatively stable over time and relatively easy to monitor. Some schools have no record of

the educational level of the parents and choose not to try to get this information. These schools have generally relied on eligibility for free or reduced-price lunches. This indicator will work, but it is less reliable, especially when it is used with middle-grade students and above, who often do not utilize the lunch program.

Gender, race/ethnicity, and socioeconomic status are often referred to as "the big three" and therefore ought not to be overlooked unless there is a compelling reason for doing so.

Other Demographic Variables

Once the faculty understands the principle of disaggregation, they will become comfortable with using it as a tool to answer many important questions about who is benefiting or not benefiting from the instructional program. Later, they may wish to suggest additional variables for disaggregation. Some more common examples might be average attendance, number of years at the school, specific school program (e.g., college bound), and many others. These variables can be very useful in informing the school about important factors related to student success.

Whatever variables are selected by the faculty to give focus to student outcomes, the faculty must be committed to monitoring them *over time*. Only data collected over time—or **trend data**—can tell us whether our school improvement strategies are having the desired impact on these populations.

Common Questions about Data Disaggregation

Should student outcomes to be disaggregated be restricted to test scores?

The data to be disaggregated need not be limited to test scores. Data could include teacher ratings of work completed (e.g., project grades); attendance figures, student attitudes, etc. If the data meet the minimum essentials of measurement (reliability and validity), and if they are inclusive of all students, they may be good candidates for disaggregation.

In the Effective Schools process, the concept of "curriculum mastery" is important. How is this concept defined, and is it a part of the disaggregation process?

"Curriculum mastery" is defined as the minimum level of student performance needed to be successful at the next grade. In some measures (such as state assessment tests) mastery standards are defined in the assessment measure itself (e.g., 75 percent of the objectives mastered). Sometimes, schools choose the median on a standardized norm-referenced test. For other measures, the standard needs to be determined locally. For example, in answering the question, "What eighth-grade math score must a student achieve before we can be confident he/she could take and pass Algebra with a C grade or better?" the answer determines the level of performance needed to predict success at the next level.

Mastery is generally associated with lower levels of achievement—minimums, the floor. What about those who worry that the top-performing students may be penalized by the Effective Schools process?

The process of disaggregation is just as useful in monitoring the achievement of top-performing students as it is in monitoring those who are struggling. For example, if 75 percent is considered minimum mastery on an assessment, one could monitor, over time, how many students score at or above 95 percent on the assessment. Using other data gathering tools (such as a survey), you can then identify whether these students are being effectively challenged and how to best meet their needs.

Our student population is small. When outcome data are disaggregated, the numbers of students are so small that they are not perceived as reliable. For example, one student may represent a total of 10 percent of a class that only has 10 boys. Is there any way to adjust for this problem of small size?

Whenever you have a population that is too small, you can consider collapsing categories across groups or across grade level. For example, Grades 1, 2, and 3 could be treated as a single group of early elementary students, and Grades 4, 5, and 6 as the upper elementary group. It would be possible to determine how well boys do in early elementary compared to later elementary programs. A similar analysis could compare the success for boys to girls.

Technology

There was a time when collecting and processing data was an arduous and time-consuming process. With the advent of computers and spreadsheet technology, it has become much easier to compile data and to perform the types of analyses that will yield accurate and useful results. Spreadsheets such as Microsoft Excel^R are invaluable in compiling and manipulating data. They allow you to disaggregate data quickly and accurately, as well as to monitor data over time. In addition, spreadsheets make displaying your data a snap, easily generating graphs and charts that make the data easily understood by all stakeholders.

There are also many education software packages that will assist you in collecting and compiling data, from the classroom level to the district level. An example of a classroom program would be Accelerated Reader™. In this program, students read a book from the AR list and take a computerized comprehension test. The teacher can then look at the scores for a particular student over time and identify those students who are struggling with reading comprehension. In addition, the student gets immediate feedback as soon as the test is completed.

With all the software options available, there is no excuse for not being "data-driven" in developing and monitoring continuous school improvement.

KEY CONCEPTS

- Measures of central tendency are most useful when describing a homogenous group.

- Measures of dispersion and variability give you a more accurate picture of the data when used in conjunction with measures of central tendency.

- In order to answer the question of equity, student outcome data must be disaggregated by the major subpopulations of the school.

- The most common variables used to disaggregate student achievement data are gender, race/ethnicity, and socioeconomic status.

- Once variables are chosen, they must be monitored over time.

- Curriculum mastery is the minimum level of student performance needed to be successful at the next level of schools.

- Technology in the form of computers, software, and Internet-based programs and services are readily available to assist in data analysis.

Chapter 10

Data-Display Tools

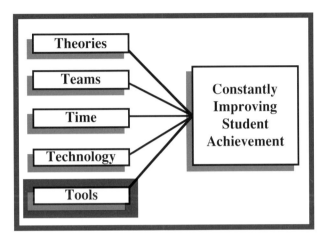

Data-driven decision making, problem solving, and continuous improvement planning requires two essential ingredients: good data and stakeholder collaboration. To qualify as good data, the information needs to be collected with great care, using fair and accurate procedures. Furthermore, data-driven decision making by a collaborative group requires that the data be communicated in such a way that all the collaborating stakeholders understand what is being communicated.

The appropriate data collection and analysis procedures were presented and discussed in the previous chapters. This chapter will focus on the general issue of how to display data for the stakeholders that assures their understanding of the data and what conclusions can be drawn from it.

Entire books, graduate courses, and computer software programs have been devoted to the art and science of data display. If you and your colleagues have not had the benefit of some training, it would be time well-spent to increase your skills in this critical area. This chapter is not intended to make you an expert; it is designed to share some guidelines and discuss a few more common applications in the continuous school improvement area.

Guidelines for Displaying Data

Those who have found themselves in a position of preparing written reports or PowerPoint[R] presentations, or generally communicating data as information to be broadly understood, know many of the practical suggestions that follow.

Keep It Simple

The most common mistake that is made when attempting to communicate data in a table, graph, or chart is including too much information. When too much information is "crammed" into one source, readers often get confused, lost, and frustrated. As a result, communication for understanding fails.

Provide Necessary Information

Even when the amount of information to be displayed is appropriate for the table, chart, or graph, the author must be sure to provide all the relevant facts necessary to understand what is being displayed. Good titles for tables and graphs, well-labeled variables, and color-coded lines all help the reader to locate the important finding being communicated.

Attach Footnotes When Necessary

Sometimes qualifying information needs to accompany a table, chart, or graph. Writers often include the qualifying statements in the narrative portion of the report. Unfortunately, the relevant narrative may be some distance removed from the data display itself. To be sure that confusion does not occur, the data display itself should have footnotes explaining what the reader needs to understand about the display.

Place Detailed Data In The Appendix

Often the author of the report, in wanting to avoid being accused of withholding valuable data, puts all the data in the body of the report. A better strategy is to make good decisions as to what key data should be displayed in the body of the text of the report and put any remaining data displays in the appendix.

Get Your Hands Dirty In The Data

Computer software has made it easy to create graphs, charts, and tables. Such software should be a ready tool for anyone who has to process data as a part of their role in a continuous improvement effort. However, to truly understand what is going on in the data, you should "get your hands dirty" in the data. If you do—that is, if you examine it from different points of view—you'll feel much more confident when you write your reports or present your data.

Common Data Display Tools

The old adage "a picture is worth a thousand words" holds true when trying to clearly communicate data and inform decision making. Generally speaking, data gathering yields an array of data points (e.g., scores) that have been carefully collected and reported. Data analysis procedures are used to summarize the "raw data" using appropriate statistical calculations (e.g., mean vs. median vs. mode). Data display involves communicating the results of your data analyses in such a way that large amounts of narrative can be seen in a single display. The two most widely used strategies are graphs and tables.

Graphs

Most likely a day doesn't go by that you don't see a graph of some kind. Whether on the 6:00 o'clock news, in the newspaper or a magazine, a textbook, or a report, graphs are the most common way to visually communicate data. Typically, most graphs you see on a daily basis fall under three categories: a bar graph, a line graph, or a pie chart. These graphic communicators are so common for a reason—they communicate information clearly.

Bar Graphs

There are several types of bar graphs. The simplest are vertical and horizontal bar graphs. Other specialized bar charts are the stacked bar chart, the histogram, and the Pareto chart.

The basic vertical and horizontal bar graphs can be used to display the responses of stakeholders to specific survey questions, as shown in Figure 10.1 below, or to display student achievement data such as achievement data disaggregated by subgroup, as shown in Figure 10.2.

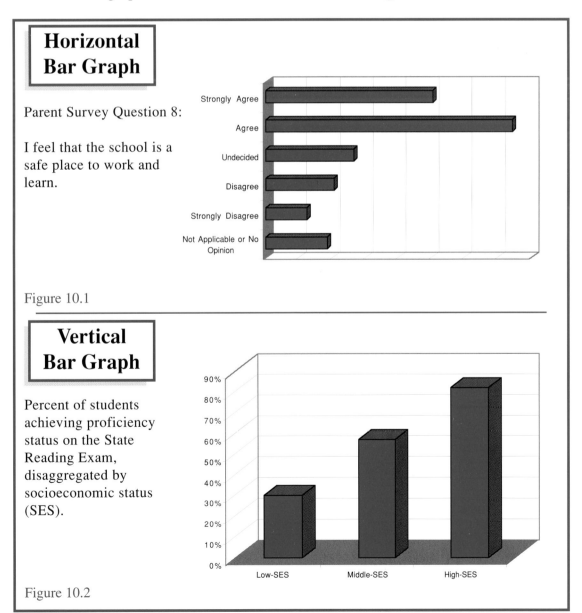

Horizontal Bar Graph

Parent Survey Question 8:

I feel that the school is a safe place to work and learn.

Strongly Agree
Agree
Undecided
Disagree
Strongly Disagree
Not Applicable or No Opinion

Figure 10.1

Vertical Bar Graph

Percent of students achieving proficiency status on the State Reading Exam, disaggregated by socioeconomic status (SES).

90%
80%
70%
60%
50%
40%
30%
20%
10%
0%

Low-SES   Middle-SES   High-SES

Figure 10.2

The stacked bar chart can be used to display data percentages in comparison to the total. For example, the stacked bar graph below shows how 4th grade boys and girls performed on two portions of the state mathematics test.

The histogram is a bar graph that uses a range of data along one axis as opposed to percentages or real numbers (i.e., 0 to 50). This is a good way to show variation in the data, particularly for process data. A histogram that indicates a process that is in line with expectations will follow the normal curve (see Chapter 9 for a discussion of the normal curve). A histogram that deviates significantly (for example, is bimodal) will communicate areas of concern despite the fact that the numerical average of the data may be in line with expectations. A good discussion of the histogram and its uses can be found in the text *Continuous Improvement Tools in Education, Volume 2* by Richard Chang and Douglas Dalziel.

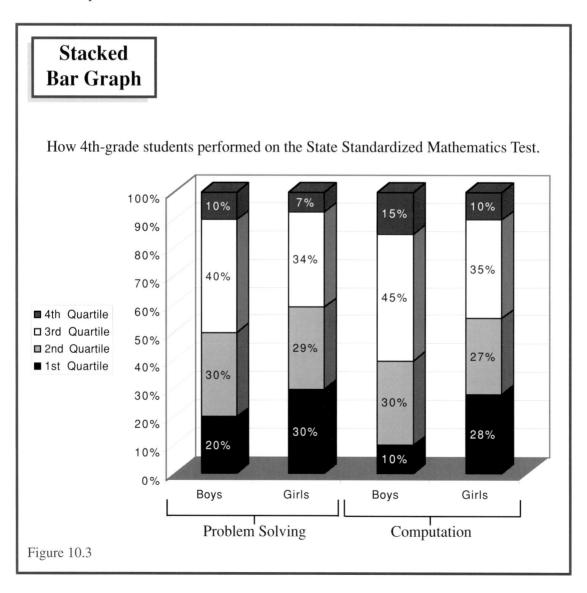

Stacked Bar Graph

How 4th-grade students performed on the State Standardized Mathematics Test.

Figure 10.3

The Pareto chart helps the leadership team to rank various problems or solutions in order of frequency or importance. Later in this book we discuss the 80/20 rule: that eighty percent of the improvement will come from 20 percent of the changes. The Pareto chart will help you identify and communicate those items that cause 80 percent of a school's problems so that all stakeholders can clearly see the priority issues. The Pareto chart below ranks parent responses to a questionnaire about the most serious problems at the school.

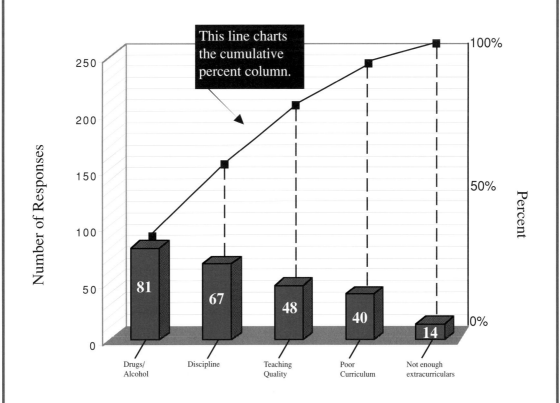

Pareto Chart

Parent Survey Question #10: What do you think is the most pressing problem facing XYZ High School?

This line charts the cumulative percent column.

(You would want to ask the same question of other stakeholder groups, e.g., teachers, students, or community members to see if there is agreement on this issue.)

Figure 10.4

Line Graphs

Basic line graphs typically allow you to display data over time, or trend data. The line graph below is called a run chart and shows weekly absences over the ten-week term for XYZ High School. You can see by the chart that the number of unexcused absences starts out high during the first week of the term, then dips and remains relatively stable for five weeks, and then begins to rise from Week 6 through the end of the term. This graph clearly communicates that there is a problem with attendance at the beginning and end of the term and can be used as a basis for further investigation as to why this might be so.

To develop a run chart:

1. Choose one key measure (e.g., student absenteeism);

2. Choose the time interval for measurement (e.g., daily attendance);

3. Draw your graph placing the measure on the vertical axis and the time interval on the horizontal axis;

4. Plot the data on the graph as you collect it;

5. Display the graph where stakeholders can view the trends that emerge.

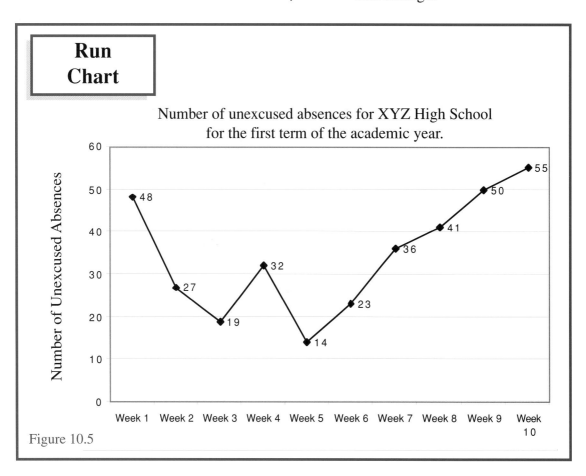

Run Chart

Number of unexcused absences for XYZ High School for the first term of the academic year.

Figure 10.5

Control Chart

A control chart takes the run chart one step further by adding a statistical analysis to let you know whether any variation in the trend is due to chance (that it falls within expected boundaries) or whether it represents a significant event or problem. It is a useful way to visually communicate the relationship between the measures of central tendency and variability.

Pie Charts

A pie chart is probably the single most common graph we encounter in our daily lives. It is used to show how a sample or population is divided among specified categories. For example, a pie chart would be useful to describe the ethnic make up of a school as shown in the figure below.

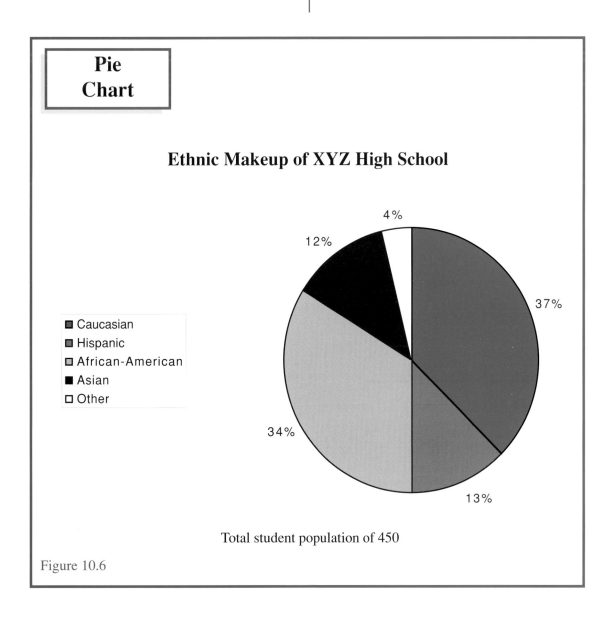

Pie Chart

Ethnic Makeup of XYZ High School

- ■ Caucasian
- ■ Hispanic
- □ African-American
- ■ Asian
- □ Other

4%
12%
37%
13%
34%

Total student population of 450

Figure 10.6

Other Types of
Graphs and Charts

Scatter Diagram

A scatter diagram (also called a "scatter plot") is a type of graph that allows you to look at the relationship between two variables. In particular, it can examine how strong a relationship is between two variables and indicate possible causal relationships. A scatter diagram can also determine the direction of the relationship (whether it is positive or negative).

To illustrate, let's take two variables that intuitively have a logical relationship, such as reading scores and history scores. We can hypothesize that students with higher reading scores will also have higher history scores because research has shown that reading for content is an essential skill to academic success in other areas. To examine this relationship we may look at the data provided us from the state standardized tests for reading comprehension and history. Using this data we create a chart with horizontal (X) and vertical (Y) axes. As a rule, we put our assumed causal factor on the horizontal axis. In our example, the (X) axis would be reading scores. The "effect" variable would be placed on the vertical axis. In this case, the (Y) axis would be history scores.

As we plot our scores, a pattern may occur. Depending on how the data clusters, the scatter diagram will indicate no relationship, a negative relationship, or a positive relationship. Below are three scatter diagrams depicting these specific outcomes.

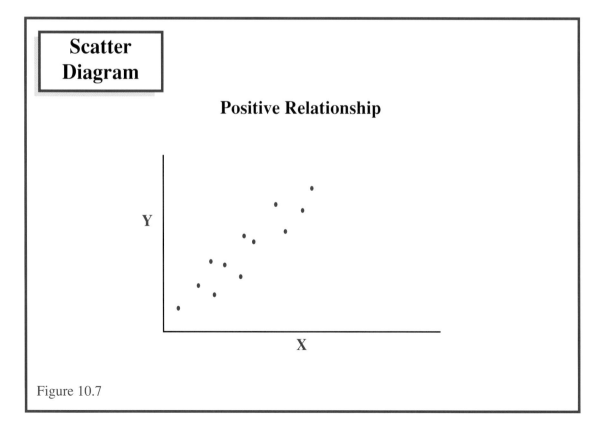

Scatter Diagram

Positive Relationship

Y

X

Figure 10.7

Scatter Diagram

Negative Relationship

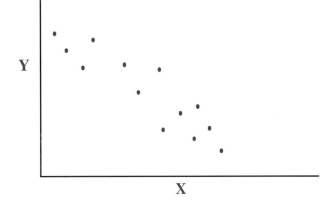

Figure 10.8

Scatter Diagram

No Relationship

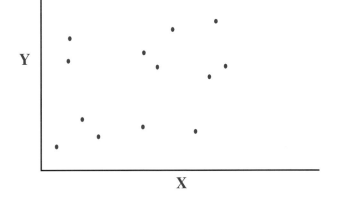

Figure 10.9

Flow Chart

Flow charts became widely used in developing computer programs decades ago. They have since found uses in all kinds of endeavors because they are extremely useful in visually communicating the steps in a process. There are a wide variety of symbols used in developing flow charts, but most often you will use rectangle and diamond shapes, along with directional arrows.

The rectangles represent process tasks, things that need to be done before the next step is taken. Diamonds represent decision-making points. Below is an example of a flow chart representing a portion of the continuous school improvement cycle.

Note: The flowchart can be used to visually communicate and evaluate the steps in a current process in addition to outlining the steps in a new process.

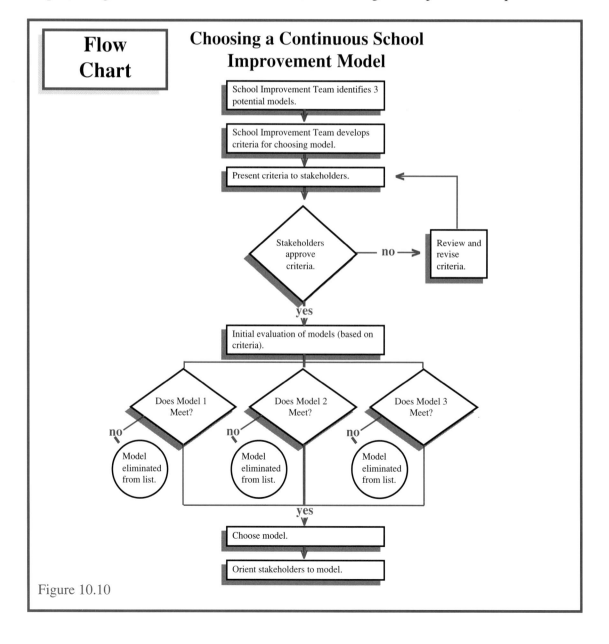

Figure 10.10

Tree Diagram

The tree diagram is a good way to both identify the strategies and tasks needed to reach a specific objective and to communicate that information to stakeholders. The tree diagram partially outlines a reading improvement program. You will see at once that it is incomplete and you could probably add quite a few steps to each level. That's one of the advantages of the tree diagram; it helps you visualize the process so you can identify any gaps that may exist. Once all the steps and strategies are identified, the information can be transferred to a Gant chart or Activity and Monitoring Matrix to allow timelines and responsibility for specific tasks to be assigned.

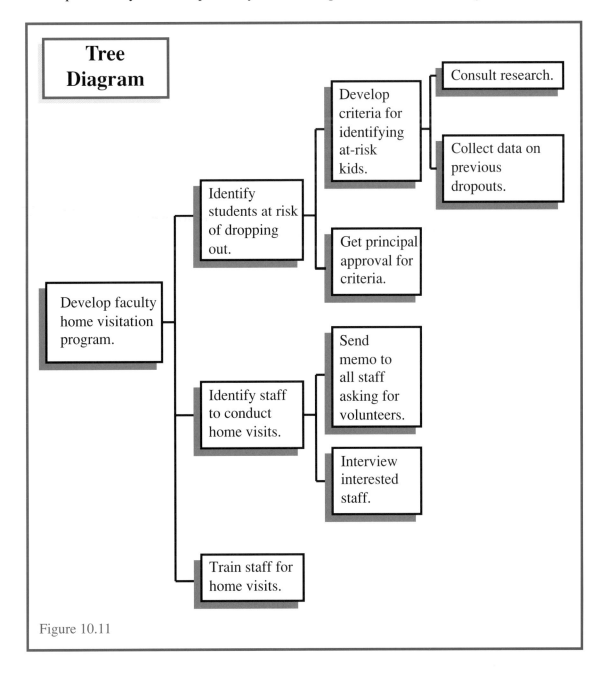

Figure 10.11

Gant Chart

A Gant chart is simply a to-do list that is charted out on a timeline that shows start and end dates for each task. Below is a Gant chart for developing the faculty home visitation program in the previous example.

Matrices

There are many variations on the matrix diagram concept. We use the matrix to provide a visual representation of who will do what task and a way to monitor progress on each task. Below is an example of a matrix.

Gant Chart

Activity	Who's Responsible	Sept.	Oct.	Nov.	Dec.	Jan.	Feb.	Mar.	Apr.	May
Research dropout criteria for at-risk students.		▇								
Review data on previous dropouts.		▇▇								
Get principal approval for criteria.			▇▇							
Identify at-risk students.			▇							
Recruit staff to conduct home visits.			▇▇▇▇							
Interview interested staff.			▇▇							
Train staff for home visits.				▇▇						
Conduct home visits.					▇▇▇▇▇▇▇					
Evaluate home visit program.								▇▇▇▇		

Figure 10.12

In a later chapter, we will specifically recommend an activity and monitoring matrix that will be useful in implementing your continuous school improvement plan.

Program Evaluation Tool

The matrix can be used to monitor progress on the objectives, including assessing both intended and unintended effects, either positive or negative.

Matrix Diagram

	Person Responsible	Task	Due Date
Task 1	John Smith	Research criteria	Mid Sept.
Task 2	Mary Jones	Review past data	Late Sept.
Task 3	Eduardo Torres	Compile report	Mid Oct.
Task 4	John Smith	Recruit staff	Mid Oct.
Task 5	Daniel Chang	Interview staff	Early Nov.
Task 6	Leadership Committee	Develop and conduct staff training	Mid Nov.

Figure 10.13

Program Evaluation Tool

Assessing the Impact of School Improvement

Goal 1. _____

CONSEQUENCES

	Intended	Unintended
I M P A C T	Positive:	Positive:
	Negative:	Negative:

What information will be collected by whom, and when, in order to monitor the impact of your action plans for each improvement goal?

Figure 10.14

KEY CONCEPTS

- The most important thing to remember when choosing graphs, charts, and other display tools is clarity. That is, does the chart tell the story?

- It's best to communicate one important concept clearly than to try to present a large amount of data at once.

- Don't make the reader look through the body of a report to find an explanation for the chart or graph. If the data need additional explanation, put it in a footnote.

Part two

CONTINUOUS SCHOOL IMPROVEMENT:
APPLYING THE 5 T'S

Part II

Continuous School Improvement: Applying the 5 T's

In the introduction to *Assembly Required*, we said that you would need the component parts, tools, and instructions to build a continuous school improvement system. Part I presented the component concepts and principles of continuous school improvement, as well as the tools that would allow you to base your efforts on a data-driven, research-based, inclusive foundation. This section will provide you the necessary "instructions" that, if followed, should enable you to create a successful and sustainable continuous school improvement system.

One of the difficult challenges in preparing the instructions for a continuous improvement system is that most schools are not starting at "ground zero." Because the pervasive pressure for school reform has existed for some time now, virtually every school has been or is now doing *something* in the name of school improvement. Just as the person assembling the swing set may have some of the necessary tools and parts, your school may indeed have some of the recommended components already in place.

We are writing **Part II** as though every reader was starting school improvement from the very beginning. That said, this publication is *not* intended to undermine or disregard good work that has been completed or is underway. If you find that some of the recommended activities have already been completed and are satisfactorily in place, feel free to skip those activities or use them with or without modification. See this as a form of affirmation and validation of your accomplishments; celebrate them, build upon them, and move on to the areas you have yet to address.

Overview of the Continuous School Improvement Process

Generally speaking, most adults have an intuitive sense of what it means to be engaged in a continuous improvement process. One of the major goals of this section is to connect the tacit knowledge most adults have with an explicit continuous improvement model, and connect both to school improvement. If this goal is achieved, those responsible for continuous improvement will share a common language rich with personal and professional metaphors.

Let us begin the conversation by using an example of continuous improvement to which everyone can relate. Suppose that you or someone close to you made a serious New Year's resolution to lose ten pounds (**MISSION**). If they were serious about achieving that goal, what would they likely do next? Most people would "weigh in" or benchmark their weight at the outset of the journey and collect data about their eating habits, perhaps by keeping a food journal (**STUDY**). Next, their attention would turn to a careful consideration of two dimensions. First, they would examine their own lifestyle (*What kinds of foods do I eat? How often do I exercise?*) to determine needed changes and then examine different approaches to making those changes, such as different kinds of diets or exercise options (**REFLECT**). The next logical step would be to develop a plan of action (select a diet and set up an exercise regimen) which, when implemented, would take the individual to the goal (**PLAN**). Finally, the individual would then implement the plan (**DO**) and begin the whole cycle again until the goal is achieved.

The steps in this intuitive continuous improvement cycle are the same as those outlined in the continuous improvement literature as the Shewhart Cycle, named after the individual credited with its development. Our adaptation of the Shewhart Cycle will be used as the "core technology" of our approach to continuous school improvement. In the final chapters of this book, we will examine each of the steps of the cycle in some depth and suggest strategies to aid you in your efforts.

But before we examine each step, there are some things you and the leadership team must do to prepare the way for continuous school improvement. Like a hiker that packs for a long trek up a mountain—an apt metaphor for schools beginning the school improvement process—you and your school improvement team must take time to prepare yourselves and all the stakeholders for this arduous process. First, you must establish the process as collaborative and inclusive from the very beginning (remember, those who are involved in the process are more likely to be supportive). Second, you must begin the work of continuous improvement with the schools, mission, core beliefs, and core values clearly articulated and widely shared by the stakeholders. Third, you must ensure that the school improvement process is being undertaken for the right reasons; that is, you must ensure that the process is focused on student learning at high levels (instructional focus).

Each step in Part II is designed to build the school's capacity to conduct continuous and sustainable school reform. We will focus on the school team as the agent of change, and, using the theories and tools presented in Part I, accomplish two objectives. The first three chapters of this section will help you lay the groundwork for fundamental change at the school level by addressing the steps listed above: including the important stakeholders; clarifying your mission, values, and beliefs; and assuring instructional focus. We will then use the modified Shewhart Cycle (Study > Reflect > Plan > Do) in conjunction with the tools and theories to help you develop a blueprint for building a continuous school improvement system for your school that will result in better teaching and learning and higher student achievement.

Chapter 11

Getting Ready for Continuous Improvement

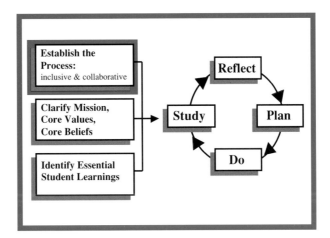

In his book, *Creating the Corporate Future*, author and systems scholar, Russell Ackoff, introduces us to a change model called Idealized Redesign of a System. The essence of this approach to change starts by asking the stakeholders of the current system the following question. Imagine that the current system (school or school district) was completely destroyed last night and you and your colleagues were asked to redesign and rebuild the system without constraint (political, legal, or fiscal). Given the aim of the systems, what would you do different?

According to Ackoff, Idealized Redesign—as a process—must meet three standards. The redesigned system must be **feasible**, **sustainable**, and **adaptable**. Here we add a fourth standard; it must be **transportable**. Feasibility means that we have the knowledge to create the new system we envision. To be sustainable, the new system must be

able to be kept going indefinitely. A redesigned system that has the capacity to "learn from its own experiences" can be considered adaptable. Finally, the new system is transportable if it has broad application and can be effectively implemented in various venues.

This model for continuous school improvement meets these four standards and serves as an example of idealized redesign of a school. As we specified earlier, the model is based on three theoretical perspectives: Effective Schools Research, Systems Theory, and Total Quality Management/Continuous Improvement. The fact that this model has been successfully implemented in many schools and districts over many years is evidence that the model meets the feasibility and sustainability standards.

Furthermore, the lessons learned in many of the schools and districts that have used this approach, and the documented adjustments they made, illustrates the system's capacity to learn from its own experience. Finally, the model has been successful in urban and rural schools, schools with varying ethnic and racial populations and socioeconomic status, and across geographic locations. This broad success, regardless of the characteristics of the school or district, confirms the model's transportability.

Whose idea is this anyway?

This model of continuous improvement depends heavily on internal commitment, ownership, and support by the school or district's many stakeholder groups. After all, as the process unfolds, *they* will be the ones who must change as part of the implementation strategy. This being so, we start off with the proverbial "chicken

---

Grading Your School

On the following scale, give your current school or school system's current school improvement efforts a "grade" for Russell Ackoff's Idealized Redesign criteria.

Criteria	Weak		Moderate		Strong
1. Feasibility	1	2	3	4	5
2. Sustainability	1	2	3	4	5
3. Adaptability	1	2	3	4	5

For each criteria to which you gave your school or school system a low mark, please explain briefly why.

_____

_____

_____

Leadership Team Challenge:

Brainstorm ideas how you could redesign your school or district's school improvement efforts to move it toward the ideal.

_____

_____

_____

Figure 11.1

versus egg" dilemma. On the one hand, if the model is perceived as being imposed on the stakeholders, there will be more resistance downstream. On the other hand, many staff will have neither the time nor desire to do the necessary research to make an informed opinion about this or other possible approaches to continuous and sustainable school reform. Furthermore, those familiar with the current system are probably pretty comfortable with the way things are and may not be eager to deliberately disrupt them. Resolving this dilemma successfully should be viewed as a matter of utmost importance. What guidance can we offer?

If the stakeholders can't say "no," then saying "yes" doesn't mean anything. But how do we reconcile this with the need to improve our schools? The key, then, is to provide a menu of choices to all stakeholders that give them control over their own participation and input into the process itself, but does not inhibit the process.

Maintaining the status quo is **not** an option.

We begin by announcing that we are embarking on a journey of school improvement, and that this journey is not optional for our school, district, and even state. Given the general climate of expectation for school reform, such a declaration should come as no surprise to anyone. At this point, staff who have a professional or moral objection to school improvement may choose to explore other career options or at least other schools or districts.

Choosing a direction, getting everyone on board.

We can now begin to use the collaborative process to build commitment and ownership. The first step centers on how to best pursue the goal of continuous school improvement in our setting. If we are talking about a single school, the principal and a small, representative cross-section of the other stakeholder groups should be empowered to go on a "scouting expedition" to examine the various available models. Their goal will be to come back to the broader stakeholder groups with a specific recommendation accompanied by supporting rationale. Before the scouts proceed, they should take the time to develop the criteria against which to judge the various models that are to be considered. For example, the team may judge the models as to whether they are:

1. Research-based
2. Data-driven
3. Results-oriented
4. Focused on quality and equity
5. Collaborative-in-form
6. Ongoing and self-renewing

These are key components to successful school reform and form the basis of the model presented here. However, the team may want to add to, delete, or modify these criteria. It may take some time and discussion to reach a reasonable level of consensus, but it will be time well spent. As a matter of fact, it would be wise to take the criteria before the larger stakeholder communities for affirmation. This will serve to strengthen the base of support for the team's efforts and final recommendation.

Certainly, it is much more expedient for the principal to announce that this or that model is going to be used, end of discussion. The problem comes later when we need to call upon the energies that will only come and be sustained through authentic commitment. Even under the best of circumstances, sustainable change of individuals and institutions is difficult. Experience has taught us that building a broad base of support for the model itself goes a long way in creating positive and high expectations that participants will, in fact, do what the model ultimately calls them to do.

Identifying the Important Stakeholders

Use the chart below to identify the primary stakeholders who should be involved in your school or district's continuous school improvement process.

Stakeholder Group	Why Chosen? What is that group's interest? What motivates them to want to be involved in your school's improvement efforts?
1. _____	Why? _____
2. _____	Why? _____
3. _____	Why? _____
4. _____	Why? _____
5. _____	Why? _____
6. _____	Why? _____
7. _____	Why? _____
8. _____	Why? _____

Figure 11.2

We are already doing our best!

When asked, most adults will readily admit to the fact that they have to remodel or redecorate their homes from time to time. They see such renewal as a natural part of home ownership. They do not see the need to redecorate as accusing them of being bad homeowners or otherwise negligent.

Take the same adults and call upon them to engage in a school improvement effort. If they are schoolteachers or administrators, they will likely get upset and defensive and interpret this call for school improvement as suggesting that they have not been doing a good job, or that they have been derelict in their professional duties. To be fair, this attitude has been inflamed by the increasing politicization of education and the penchant for our society to place blame. However, for the school reform process to be successful, leadership must mitigate this perception.

We know that the knowledge base of teaching and learning is always changing, that learners aren't the same today as in the past, that the curricular content is different, and that new technologies are creating problems and opportunities unheard of just a few years ago. The effective leader will make it clear that improvements are needed because of the changing societal context, educational mission, and expected level of learning. Help your colleagues to see that it is not about them "playing the game poorly"— it's about the fact that *the game itself has changed*.

Sometimes resistance to improvement and change is used to disguise the doubts that many educators have about their own competence or ability to successfully manage the change. Any and all efforts to reassure staff that they will receive the necessary training and technical assistance will be central to the change process. It may also be necessary to reassure staff that their jobs are secure. Be careful not to make this promise unless the local Board of Education will support this policy.

Completing the Preparation Stage

Let's assume that, after careful reflection, the scouting team decides to recommend this model as the framework for their school or district's improvement efforts. What happens next?

Stakeholder Orientation to the Continuous Improvement Model

Adopting the Continuous School Improvement Model should represent an informed decision by the majority of the stakeholders. To achieve the necessary levels of information, all stakeholders should have an opportunity to participate in an orientation program. The primary goal of this orientation is to present the model, introduce its history and research base, and provide examples of successful case studies. The stakeholders need to be "schooled" in the language of the model and be given an opportunity to discuss their questions and concerns.

The orientation can take many forms and be elaborate or simple and straightforward. The steering committee will decide the best approach for their school or district. In some schools, the orientation calls for study groups to read and present their findings to the stakeholders. In other situations, the steering committee organizes a presentation and facilitates discussions designed to solicit the stakeholders' issues and concerns.

An important goal of the orientation process is for the stakeholder groups to understand the role of the leadership team in initiating and sustaining continuous school improvement. While the principal plays a vital role as the instructional leader of the school, sustainable school reform requires a broad coalition of support from the various stakeholder groups.

> Leadership teams that include representatives of the various stakeholder groups, including the principal, have been found to be the most successful strategy for building ownership, commitment, and sustainability into the improvement process.

Once the stakeholder groups understand the continuous improvement process and the central role to be played by the collaborative leadership team, we can now move to the next step.

Select a School Improvement Leadership Team

In selecting the school improvement leadership team, the goal is clear: to assemble an empowered leadership team with the authority and credibility to lead the desired changes in the school or district. Achieving the goal requires decisions that are best made in context.

One key strategy is to select a representative cross-section from the various stakeholder groups so that each group feels that it has credible voice on the team. One way to assess whether this has been achieved would be to ask the question: *Could any stakeholder group not represented on the team undermine the work of the team on the grounds it was not represented?* If the answer is "no," it would be reasonable to assume that you have involved all the important stakeholder groups.

Now for the more difficult question: *What process should we use to select the individual members of the school team?* This question is both difficult and extremely important. If the processes used to select the representatives are perceived to be inappropriate, the work of the team itself will be questioned.

- **Size.** The team should be large enough to assure that it is representative, but not so large as to make it nearly impossible for the entire group to find a time to meet. A reasonable size for the school team would be five to eight members, including the principal. We would suggest that about half of the members be selected by and from the certified members of the staff, one position be reserved for noncertified staff, and two positions be earmarked for individuals representing parents and the community. However, as we noted in the chapter on teams, a larger team may be necessary to accommodate the political climate.

- **Selecting Team Members.** There are some general rules of thumb for selecting team members. First, the individuals chosen to be on the team should be positive about the school and the need for change. Resist the temptation to use membership on the school team as a rehabilitation strategy for resistant individuals. The work of sustainable change is hard enough on team members without burdening them with the most negative members of the school or district community. Second, whenever possible, the members of the team should include the opinion leaders in the school, such as those teachers who are the most respected by their colleagues, teachers who have the influence to make or break an innovation. These individuals can be instrumental in the success of the process and the initial school team selection should include at least one or two such individuals.

Secure Training for the School Leadership Team

The non-school world seems to be much further along in working productively in teams when compared to education. The school has been described as a lonely place to work; the culture of most schools historically has not provided much opportunity or encouragement for teachers to network and dialog with other teachers about professional issues.

Because of this rather dismal history, the creation of a school improvement

leadership team does not, in and of itself, make the members competent in working effectively and efficiently as a team. Therefore, team members should participate in training on how to function as a team. There are recognized strategies that can be taught that, when used, allow the team process to proceed efficiently, with a minimum of personal conflict. Refer to the chapter on teams for a list of specific skills for team members.

Efforts to implement site-based management or shared decision-making models have often faltered because no training was provided and no rules were developed that could guide the process. One good teacher quit her school team because, from her perspective, all the team ever did was talk, never making decisions or taking action. This and similar problems can be avoided with appropriate training.

Finding Time for School Improvement

Earlier, we spoke about the 5 T's, one of which was time. Whenever educators are asked to indicate the greatest barrier or obstacle to school-based improvement, the most frequent answer is "finding time to meet." Time is often a code word for money—if you want more of my time, it is going to cost more money. At one level, this is true of all professionals. If you need a lot of time from your attorney, it is going to cost you more money.

To secure quality time from the members of the leadership team, some form of incentive or compensation is desirable. For example, if a school or district can afford to provide direct compensation they should do so. This would provide clear evidence of the importance and value that the school or district attaches to the work of the leadership team.

If direct compensation is not an option, other forms of "payment" should be explored. For example, team members could be given release time, supported to attend national conferences, or provided meals. The school district needs to find manageable but fair ways to recognize the added burden that comes with being an active and contributing member of the leadership team. Chapter 6 discusses the various methods other schools and districts have used to free up staff time.

Once the members of the school leadership team have been selected, develop and announce a calendar of scheduled meeting times. The calendar is important for two reasons. First, it serves to establish the leadership team's work as important. Schools live or die by the calendar they create. Important events (e.g., vacation days) are always a formal part of the calendar because they are important. We need to do whatever seems reasonable to elevate the work of the school team and their meetings to a high priority.

Second, the calendar is important in maintaining an air of openness and inclusion. All meetings of the school leadership team should be open to any and all members of the various stakeholder groups. Furthermore, the agenda for a forthcoming meeting should be made public before every meeting. This gives those individuals who have a particular interest in an agenda item an opportunity to attend the meeting and participate in the conversation. It may turn out that no non-team members of the stakeholder communities ever attend a team meeting. While this may be disappointing, it would not be fatal to the school improvement process. What could be fatal is for the leadership team to be perceived as conducting their work in secret.

Creating an Open, Two-way Communication System

A general rule of thumb is that whoever is not in on what you're doing from the beginning is likely to be down on what you do later. Open meetings represent one strategy for avoiding this potential pitfall. In addition, the leadership team must design and announce a two-way communications plan. The plan should make it clear to everyone involved that they will be kept informed of all the deliberations of the team and will have a means by which they can provide opinions, ask questions, and express concerns.

Technology can provide a valuable tool for supporting a two-way communications plan. For example, a school or district could develop a school improvement Web page where the minutes of meetings and other pertinent materials could be posted. Tools that provide online polling could be used from time to time to gauge reactions to the issues being discussed. Finally, e-mail could be used to create "chat rooms" in which ongoing exchanges could take place.

A technology tool that is available for this type of two-way communication is an online service called the Effective Schools League™. A school with a local community on the Effective Schools League in which each staff member has a password would have access to all the tools described above.

Finally, in addition to a calendar of meeting times for the leadership team itself, time will be needed for the team to meet with the whole faculty. These meetings may be to inform the faculty about selected issues that are being considered, to provide actual training, or to provide a progress report.

Because faculty meeting time is a scarce resource in most schools, it needs to be protected and used wisely. The efficient and productive use of this time should be seen as a priority by the leadership team. To that end, it would be helpful to develop and publish a timeline so that all involved will be aware of the complexity of the process. There will then be no surprises! Because teachers and administrators are simultaneously going about the business of schooling, don't expect the planning stages to be accomplished in just a few months; it is not uncommon for the process to take anywhere from 12 to 18 months. The timeline in the appendix is meant to be a general guideline only; how quickly your school progresses through the process depends on logistical, political, staffing, and financial variables.

KEY CONCEPTS

You are now prepared to begin the difficult work of sustainable school reform. Let's review our accomplishments to date.

- The school or district community has made an informed decision to proceed with this model of continuous and sustainable school improvement.

- Every member of a stakeholder group has been given an opportunity to learn about the model and the processes involved.

- A representative team has been empowered by the larger community to lead change in the school or district.

- The importance of the work of the team has been signaled through the announced schedule of team meetings and the team with the faculty.

- The importance of each member of the school community is recognized by the fact that they are going to be kept informed and their input is going to be solicited as the process unfolds.

We have all heard the expression, "the medium is the message." The processes and the people selected to lead them represent the "medium" for this model of school improvement. How the team conducts itself relative to the others who will have to own and implement the changes is at least as critical to the long-term success of the change process as the activities themselves. Care should be taken to make sure that the "launch" of the school improvement process is the best that it can be. The downstream benefits will be apparent.

Chapter 12

Clarifying School Mission, Core Beliefs, and Core Values

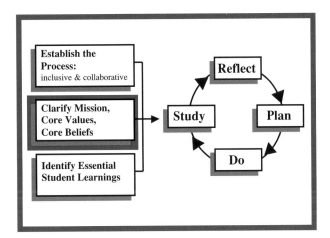

Effective school improvement is created by passion that is grounded in the mission the school community has set. When asked, most school principals will say that their school does indeed have a mission statement. But, unfortunately, too many schools assume that everyone associated with the school shares a sense of the school mission and are committed to it. But there is a world of difference between having a mission statement and having *a sense of mission*.

The difference can be described as the extent to which the mission statement elicits something akin to an emotional reaction among the members of the school community. Therefore, this chapter is designed to encourage schools to engage in deliberate and intentional processes designed to do two things:

• Clarify the mission of the school.

• Engender as much passion and commitment to its fulfillment as possible from all stakeholders.

As important as it is to be clear about and committed to the mission, it is equally important for the school to be clear about its core beliefs and core values.

A school's core beliefs and core values provide the important context for pursuing the mission. As we begin setting improvement goals and designing action plans, the school's mission, core values, and beliefs provide important criteria for selecting what strategies, tactics, and behaviors the school will implement.

In Chapter 3, we introduced you to our adaptation of Gareth Morgan's double loop learning model within the context of new knowledge. This is a critical concept to continuous and sustainable school improvement. You

Figure 12.1

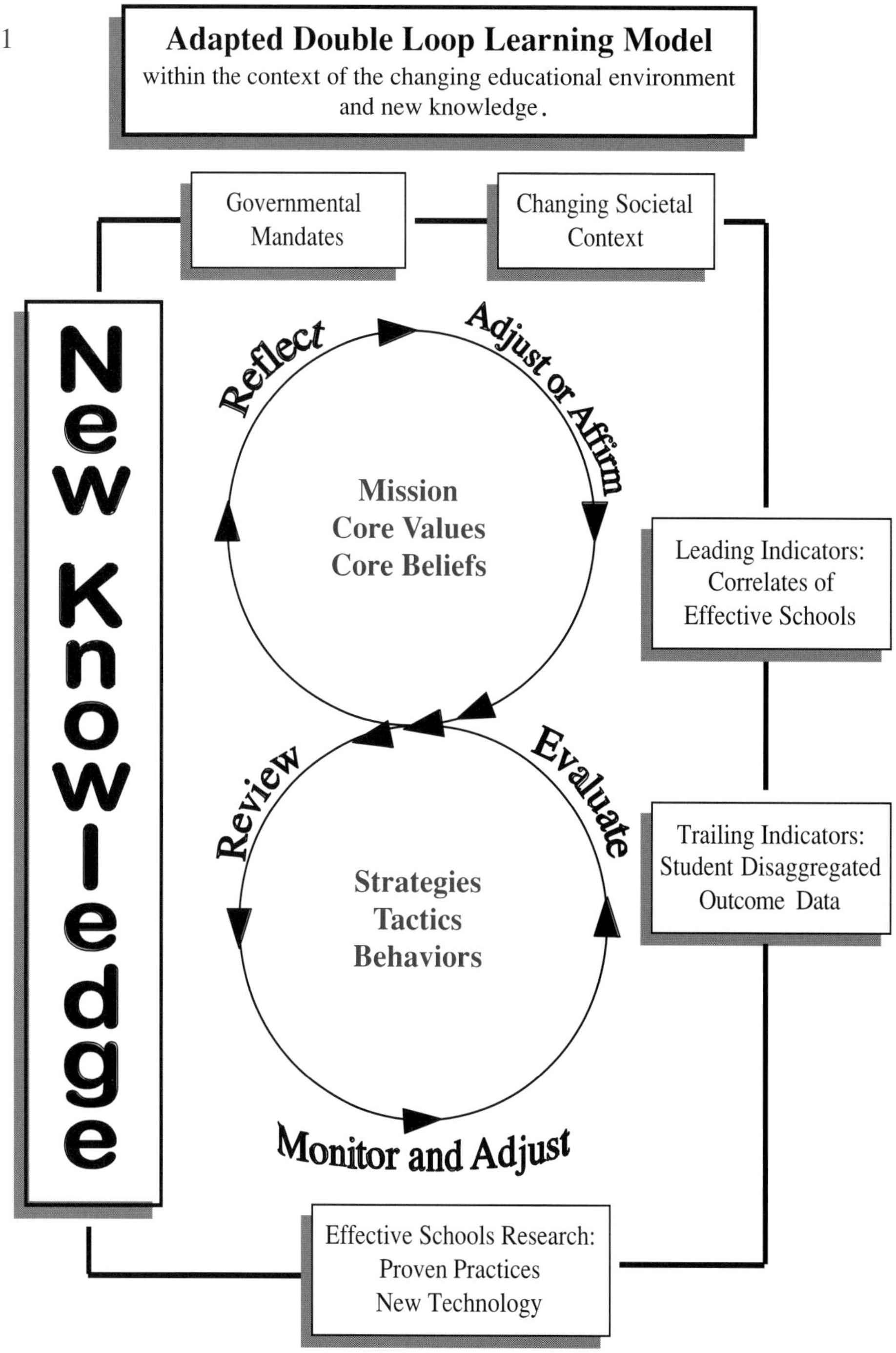

Adapted Double Loop Learning Model
within the context of the changing educational environment
and new knowledge.

Governmental Mandates

Changing Societal Context

New Knowledge

Reflect   *Adjust or Affirm*

**Mission
Core Values
Core Beliefs**

Leading Indicators:
Correlates of
Effective Schools

Review   *Evaluate*

**Strategies
Tactics
Behaviors**

Trailing Indicators:
Student Disaggregated
Outcome Data

Monitor and Adjust

Effective Schools Research:
Proven Practices
New Technology

Examples of questions to ask about mission, core beliefs, and core values:

- What do we believe?
- Do our core beliefs and values support the stated mission?
- Does our mission reflect the current input of all relevant stakeholders?
- Does our mission specify what learner outcomes are important to us and who is accountable for those outcomes?
- Are current strategies, tactics, and behaviors consistent with the current mission, core beliefs, and core values?

will recall that there are two loops in the model. The top loop equates with an organization's core values and core beliefs. The lower loop of the figure eight reflects the tactics, strategies, and behaviors used by the organization to pursue its mission and live its core values and beliefs.

Most people that are unfamiliar with Systems Theory believe that increased success on the mission only requires change in the system's tactics, strategies, or behaviors found in the lower loop. For example, many educators still cling to the belief that the solution to any learning problem in their school requires a new program. New programs, for the most part are lower-loop solutions.

Morgan, Senge, and other systems theorists argue that 80 percent of the problems in most organizations exist in the upper loop of the model. If we assume that the systems theorists are correct, any attempt to create a continuous and sustainable school improvement system must examine its core values and core beliefs as part of its effort to clarify the mission itself.

Let's begin by identifying what we mean when we speak of mission, core beliefs and core values.

Mission

The mission of a school is a short statement that indicates what that school is seeking to do, where it is attempting to go. For example, the mission statement most often associated with the Effective Schools approach to school reform is,

"learning for all—whatever it takes." Clearly, this mission statement would require further elaboration of the key terms *all*, *learning*, or *whatever it takes*. A glossary of terms could be developed to meet this need.

The mission statement should be able to respond to questions like *What is this school trying to accomplish? Where is this school trying to go?* A mission statement is **not** supposed to be a description of current reality in the school. Instead, the mission statement should describe a preferred future. It should be a "reach statement," an "aspiration statement" that can move the institution or organization beyond the moment and toward the intended future.

Core Beliefs

The strategies, tactics, and behaviors that are apparent in the day-to-day working of a school are the observable manifestation of the underlying beliefs and values of that school. The beliefs represent assumptions schools make about such important questions and issues as:

- The role of schools and schooling in a democratic society.

- How children learn and what teachers and teaching can contribute.

- How schools and other social institutions, such as family, positively or negatively impact student learning.

• The role, rights, and responsibilities of students, teachers, administrators, support staff, and parents.

Needless to say, these questions represent only a few of the deeper issues and assumptions that a school may wish to explicitly incorporate into its belief statement. The following example provided by Hillsdale Community Schools, Hillsdale, Michigan, will give you some additional ideas.

Once a belief statement is adopted, all subsequent decisions and actions should be consistent with these beliefs or the credibility of the school will be called into question.

Why is it so important to identify core beliefs? To illustrate how critical this step is to continuous school improvement, let's focus on the following belief about human learning itself. Do we believe that virtually all learning is an act of choice on the part

---

Core Beliefs Example

Hillsdale Community Schools
Hillsdale, Michigan

Beliefs that Guide Us

Education is a Shared Responsibility—achievement requires the commitment and participation of staff, students, family, and community.

All Students Can Learn—all students have potential that can be developed.

Rates of Learning Vary—the time required for mastery has no bearing on the value of the learner.

All Students Have Unique Skills and Talents—individual abilities must be identified and nurtured.

High Self-Esteem Enhances Success—people develop best through sincere praise and validation.

School Climate Contributes to Achievement—learning occurs best in an environment of mutual respect.

High Expectations for Success Must be the Norm—failure only occurs when one stops trying.

Trust is Vital—trust bonds staff, students, family, and community.

Cooperation is Essential—learning experiences must encourage and teach skills which develop a cooperative attitude.

Optimism is Critical—optimism about people, education, and the future serves all of us best.

Figure 12.2

of the learner? If this represents a core belief for our school, then our tactics, strategies, and behaviors designed to promote learning must build on student interest and active participation and minimize more coercive approaches to student motivation. For teachers and administrators who do not share that belief, building approaches to classroom lessons that strive for authentic student engagement and not simply passive compliance would be a challenge indeed.

Core Values

Core values define how we will act toward one another within our organization. For example, a core value for a school might be that every member of the school community should show respect for self, others, and the environment. If that is a cherished value for our school, we can imagine a variety of tactics, strategies, and behaviors that would come to define the culture and climate of our school.

Core values identify the behaviors that the school is committed to acting upon. That is to say, a school would strive to recognize and reward those behaviors by staff and students that illustrate the core values. Likewise, the school would develop and fairly implement sanctions for those who would behave in ways that violate the institution's core values.

Developing the Mission, Core Values, and Core Beliefs

The responsibility for designing and implementing the processes to produce the school's mission is vested in the leadership team. What follows are a set of procedural guidelines and suggested tools that can be used to complete this task.

Step 1: Laying the Groundwork.

The school leadership must remember that the task is to create a sense of mission, not simply to write a mission statement. Further, the leadership team needs to be reminded that the school, unless it is a freestanding charter, exists as a part of a larger nested system, i.e., the school district and the state in which it resides. This means that the school's mission is constrained by the larger organizational system context. To use an absurd example to demonstrate this point, a school could not decide to go out of the education business and start manufacturing radios. Its new "mission" would be incompatible with the larger system.

Therefore, creating a sense of mission in a school must begin with a clear understanding of the mission, core values, and core beliefs of the system to which it belongs. The leadership should gather the mission statements of its state and school district and analyze them. This task will give the group important insight into what is expected of them as a school and what they are prohibited from doing given the core values of the state and district.

Step 2: Engaging the Stakeholders.

Once the background research has been completed it is time to engage the various stakeholder groups in a series of conversations around the mission, core values, and core beliefs. The involvement of the stakeholders brings different perspectives to the process; it also helps to build broad-based commitment and support for the end product. Remember, involvement leads to commitment most of the time. To put this principle into practice, the leadership group should plan a two-tiered discussion with a broad representation of the various stakeholder groups.

The first discussion would be designed to get as many ideas and thoughts as possible. We recommend that the leadership team work with small, cross-sectional groups of stakeholders to solicit as many ideas as possible. In this initial discussion, we want to encourage diversity in ideas—get everything out on the table. The data gathering tools presented in Part I will expedite the group's work. Specifically, the brainstorming tool would be most appropriate here. A facilitator should be appointed to ensure that the tools are clearly understood and the processes do not get derailed.

One of the guiding theories of the Continuous School Improvement Model—the Effective Schools Framework—offers two questions that will help guide the discussion of the mission. "What is it that we want our students to know and be able to do?" (Effective at what?) and "From which students do we expect this learning?" (Effective for whom?) These questions should be answered in the mission statement and subsequently reflected in the identified essential student learnings.

Mission statements vary in their wording and format. However, each mission statement should answer the following questions, which are really more specific components of the two core questions posed above.

- Who will *deliver* the service?
- Who will *benefit*?
- What is the *nature* of the service?
- What constitutes *observable evidence* that the service has been effectively provided?
- What is the *level of accountability?*

The following mission statement has been adapted from one developed by a high school staff and illustrates how to incorporate the above questions:

XYZ High School is dedicated to assuring that students and educators are prepared for the challenges that lie ahead. We will assure exemplary education for all our students, support growth for the professionals, and foster the development of the entire educational community. Specifically, we will:

- *Teach for understanding to enable students to achieve mastery of essential skills and learn for a lifetime.*

- *Organize the school and its classrooms as a community of learning.*

- *Hold these ambitious learning goals for everybody's children.*

- *Teach adults as well as children.*

- *Make reflection and inquiry a central feature of the school.*

Q: Who will deliver the service?
A: XYZ High School

Q: Who will benefit?
A: "all our students"; "professionals"; "the entire educational community"; "everybody's children"; "adults as well as children."

Q: What is the nature of the service?
A: "assuring that students and educators are prepared for the challenges that lie ahead."

Q: What constitutes observable evidence?
A: "achieve mastery of essential skills"; "growth for professionals"; "reflection and inquiry a central feature of the school."

Q: What is the level of accountability?
A: "We will assure exemplary education for all our students, support growth for the professionals in our school, and foster the development of the entire educational community."

Step 3: Distilling the Content, Identifying the Important Components.

The completion of Step 2 yields a "laundry list" of statements that could be adopted as the mission, the statement of core values and core beliefs. Step 3 is designed to distill the list to its critical essence and build consensus around the resulting statements of mission, core values, and beliefs.

Once the brainstorming step has been completed, the leadership team should begin the process of categorizing the responses. The Affinity Diagram is an excellent process to cluster similar responses. Once the categories have been formed, the leadership team then takes on the delicate task of writing an initial draft of the mission, core values, and beliefs. The goal here is to "capture" the ideas offered by the larger group while eliminating repetition and distilling the language to clearly represent the key concepts generated by the larger group.

An excellent method for doing this is to take the list of statements from Step 2 before an expanded stakeholder group. In this conversation, each participant will have equal influence in the process. For example, each participant may be given 100 points to allocate across a list of belief statements. Participants will then be asked to assign a weight to each statement making sure to use the full allotment of points. They may give many points to some statements and few or no points to others. Sometimes participants are instructed to give no more than half the allotted points to any one statement. The assigned weight should reflect the extent to which that individual agrees with and supports the statement. The points are then added up and the statements with the most points are those that reflect the priorities of the group as a whole. And because the process was inclusive and collaborative, participating stakeholders will be able to commit to the mission, core belief, and core value statements that result from the process.

The leadership team will find it both necessary and desirable to edit the statements so that the meaning and importance of each is as clear as possible. For example, the original brainstorming of the mission statement and the subsequent synthesis may find that two critical ideas need to be reflected in the school's mission statement. Here is an example of a single statement that creatively merges two very important ideas.

"Our goal is to have all of our students do well **and** do good."

When the glossary of terms was developed to help explain the terms and phrases in the mission statement, doing well was associated with traditional measures of student achievement. The phrase "do good" was associated with public service and civic responsibility.

Step 4: Securing Broader Stakeholder Understanding and Commitment.

Steps 1 through 3 have been designed to produce a written document that includes input from a broad cross-section of the stakeholders, and "cooks it down" to a more manageable document without losing the commitment that has been engendered along the way. The fourth step in the process is to have the work of the leadership team and the others ratified by all the members of the stakeholder groups. All teachers, administrators, support staff, parents, and perhaps students (high school level) should be given an opportunity to review the resulting mission, core belief and core value statements and discuss the meaning behind each.

A mission statement may go through many revisions until a version emerges that can be wholeheartedly embraced by the majority of the stakeholders. It is critical to take the time necessary for open and free discussion so that all who

are interested can participate and contribute their opinions and ideas. This will only serve to increase the understanding of and commitment to the mission statement.

There are many ways to solicit stakeholder comments. One way is to circulate a written draft of the statement with space for the reviewer to comment. A sample form is provided on page 128. For those who prefer to incorporate technology into the process, simply post your statement at your Web site, Effective Schools League Community, or intranet site and ask for input via e-mail or, in the case of the League, the discussion feature.

Once everyone is clear on the statements and their meanings, and all input has been solicited, considered, and incorporated where appropriate, each stakeholder group should be given an opportunity to formally ratify the document. If the orientation process reveals the need for further editing and clarification of the mission, core belief, or core value statements, take the time to do so.

Step 5: "Taking it to the Streets."

Once ratified, the statement of mission, core values and core beliefs should be used as a high profile document in all subsequent discussions and publications distributed by the school. For example, this document should be prominently displayed in the lobby of the school. It should be included in the student handbook, parent newsletters, and on display at school events like curriculum nights. If this document is going to serve as the guiding force for the school, it cannot be emphasized too much.

How do you keep your mission statement from becoming just another plaque on the wall? Once the mission statement is developed, there must be an ongoing dialogue that deepens people's understanding of it. Without such conversation, they will naturally believe that their current actions reflect the mission and not give it further thought. "People must be provided with experience that help them think more deeply about what is meant by their school's guiding statements beyond what they are already thinking and doing." (Allen, 2001) In addition, administrators must see to it that the mission is used to orient all new employees and guide all school improvement efforts. Furthermore, any new curricula, school programs, and actions should be evaluated in light of the extent to which they further the school's mission.

How long should it take to complete the mission, core values, and core beliefs document? The honest answer is, "We don't know." Some schools are already operating with a shared sense of mission and a clear understanding of its core beliefs and values even though they have never been formally written and ratified as such. A school like this probably could move quickly through the five steps and formalize the document without a lot of conversation. On the other hand, schools that have little history of conversing about such important matters as mission, beliefs, and values will likely need more time and more conversation and probably more drafts of the document. This is important work and can not be rushed. After all, if you don't have time to do it right the first time, where will you find time to fix it later?

One final thought. While the mission, values, and beliefs can be modified from time to time, they should be thought of as being relatively fixed and permanent. Like the U.S. Constitution, a school's mission, values and beliefs can and should be periodically reviewed and amended when necessary, but this is not something that should be done lightly or often.

Mission Statement Proposal Form

Date: _____

School: _____

The mission statement below was written through the collaboration of faculty and staff, parents, and the community. It is an expression of why our school exists, who we serve, and what we strive to do. Please read the mission below and answer the questions that follow.

Proposed Mission Statement:

_____

_____

_____

_____

I like the mission as it is written with no changes: ❏ YES   ❏ NO

I would like to see the following words changed:

_____

_____

I offer this version of the mission statement:

_____

_____

_____

_____

Comments:

_____

_____

Name: _____ Date: _____

Figure 12.3   (optional)

KEY CONCEPTS

- Strategies, tactics, and behaviors that are not consistent with the mission, core values, and core beliefs of an organization are doomed to fail.

- Often, organizations—especially schools—are only tacitly aware of their values and beliefs. The goal of this process is to identify and clarify these values and beliefs, and adjust or affirm them in light of the changing environment and new knowledge.

- Stakeholders who are left out of the process will be less committed to the resulting mission and may in fact erect barriers to change.

- The mission must be lived everyday. Every program, every procedure, every rule, every curriculum should be evaluated in light of the school's mission, core beliefs, and core values. Otherwise, they become just words on the wall.

- Adequate time spent here will result in solid foundation for building the Continuous School Improvement System.

Chapter 13

Assuring Instructional Focus

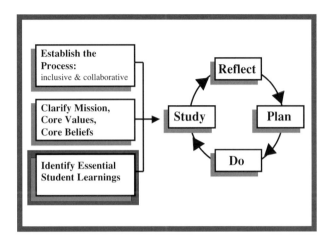

To this point, we have been silent on the curricular content to be learned in an effective school. This chapter builds the conceptual framework for the effective continuous school improvement system. Assuring instructional focus begins with two fundamental questions:

- What do the many stakeholders of the school want students to know, do and be disposed to do when they finish their time with us?

- What evidence will be gathered to assure the stakeholders that the learners know, do, and are disposed to do those things?

Where do we begin this seemingly insurmountable task? **Begin with the end in mind, design down, and deliver up.**

Let's examine the rationale behind this principle: that the goal of K-12 education is to give students as many choices as possible regarding what to do with their life when they graduate. In this sense, education is an empowerment process; it empowers the learner with choices and options. While this rationale may sound too abstract and philosophical to be practical, it really isn't. Who would argue that children who learn to read at high levels have choices and options open to them that poor readers do not? As distinguished educational scholar Ralph Tyler said many years ago, you know you are being educated when you have more choices today than you had yesterday.

Beginning with the End in Mind

If you accept this rationale, then "to begin with the end in mind" means that you will begin building the curriculum by asking "What knowledge, skills, behaviors, and dispositions provide the learners with the broadest range of choices and options when they graduate?"

The faint-of-heart may want to stop at this juncture because answering this question will require confronting a number of value choices. Implied in the question—and the answer that would follow—is the notion that, when it comes to empowering the learner with choices and options, *some things matter more than others*. Can the seemingly inevitable conflicts around value choices be avoided? Conceptually, the answer is "yes"; practically the answer is "no."

Conceptually, value conflicts could be avoided if schools had unlimited staff, time, and resources to teach all possible content. Then we could incorporate all the content that most stakeholders want. Unfortunately, the reality is that teachers have far too much content to teach, and far too little time to teach it—especially to a high standard of mastery. Therein lie the seeds of conflict.

A metaphor is useful to drive home this critical point. Let's liken the teacher to a carpenter. When the carpenter goes to a job site, he expects to find two things: a clear blueprint of the house that is to be built and sufficient raw materials to do the job. Similarly, when arriving at the job site of the classroom, a teacher has the right to expect a curricular blueprint of the job to be done and sufficient resources (e.g., time) to do it. If the job to be done is too big for the time available to do it, one of two adjustments must be made. Either the size of the job must be scaled back to fit the time available (e.g., drop grammar and teach Shakespeare), or we can go as far as we can until we run out of time (teach a little grammar and a little Shakespeare,

neither very well). Both types of accommodations are rampant in schools and classrooms today.

Returning to our carpenter metaphor once again, when the carpenter finds that the materials required by the blueprint exceeds the materials available to do it, who should be held accountable? Certainly not the carpenter! The responsible party would be the architect who drew the blueprints and ordered the materials! Clearly then, it is the responsibility of the school leadership to see that the breadth and scope of what the school is required to teach matches the time and resources available. Unfortunately, this is rarely the case.

The current misalignment between what is to be learned and the time to learn it can be solved in one of two ways. One solution would be to hold the current curricular standards constant and expand the time available to teach them. The other would be to hold the current available time constant and eliminate some of the content to be learned. Since there seems to be little interest on the part of the policymakers to put more resources forward to buy additional time, only the second strategy seems viable. The strategy of eliminating content requires deciding what will go and what will stay in the curriculum. At this point, the value conflicts many had hoped to avoid must be faced head-on.

A Process for Identifying the School's Curricular Ends

How do we choose what student learnings empower students with the maximum number of choices and options when they complete their time in school? For purposes of discussion, let us use the typical K-12 school district as the context for describing the process since the process does not change much from school to school. For K-8 district organizations, only the specified student learnings will change.

The first voice that needs to be heard when it comes to defining what we want our students to know, do, and be disposed to do upon graduation is the State in which the district resides. There are two reasons for this. First, in the United States, the Constitutional authority and responsibility for defining the aims and ends of public education is delegated to the State. In turn, most states delegate a significant portion of this authority to individual school districts. While the state can delegate authority to the local districts, the public and the courts have generally taken the position that the state cannot delegate accountability. In that sense, the teachers and administrators in the local schools are, to some degree, "agents of the state."

Second, it is only practical that the state should represent the first voice in the process of curriculum alignment because 49 of the 50 states have already developed and disseminated some form of state standards for their schools. Furthermore, the accountability and assessment systems that are a part of the current reform movement are designed to assess student performance based on state standards.

For the purposes of this narrative, we must assume that the state standards are themselves the by-product of a deliberative process designed to determine what students need to know, do, and be disposed to do when they graduate from a public high school. We can only hope that, through enough political pressure, the responsible agency has done its "homework" and developed comprehensive yet reasonable standards.

Role of the Local District and School

The state standards comprise the "floor" or minimum standards that schools must embrace. Once the state standards have been brought into the alignment discussion, then local district stakeholders must be heard. Through a collaborative process, local districts and even individual schools can add standards to student requirements. But they cannot ignore or eliminate any of the state standards.

At the end of this book you will find several examples of learner outcome statements from different schools. While each one varies in length and wording, they all clearly communicate what is expected from a high school graduate.

Selecting Student Outcomes

At any point in the process, you may end up with a list of outcomes that will require far more time and resources than is—or will be—available. Now it is time to come face-to-face with those value conflicts mentioned earlier in this chapter. How do you collaboratively determine what to leave in and what to leave out? You may want to take a survey of the stakeholders or use the criteria rating form outlined in Chapter 8 or you can adapt the form below to help you identify the curricular priorities.

Below is a list of outcomes for the _____ curriculum (e.g., social studies, science, math, English, etc.). The following exercise is designed to assist the leadership team in prioritizing those outcomes so that teachers and learners can allocate learning time accordingly.

For each column below, you have 100 points per column to distribute among the student outcomes listed. Column A indicates what you believe is the current amount of emphasis given to each outcome in your curriculum. Column B indicates the amount of emphasis you believe should be given to each outcome. Column totals should add up to 100 points exactly.

Column A Outcomes	Column B Current Emphasis	Column C Ideal Emphasis
= 100 points	= 100 points	= 100 points

Distribute this form to the relevant stakeholders. When you receive the forms back, total the points given each outcome and divide by the number of responses to find the average and rank accordingly to prioritize the list of outcomes.

Figure 13.1

Once the state, local school board, and school have defined the performance goals to be achieved upon graduation, we can now begin the process of "backward mapping" the curriculum from the agreed-upon exit goals. To start this process, we need to ask two questions of the stakeholder groups that represent the interests of the school board and the high schools.

What learning experiences do the students need *in grade twelve* so that when students leave they are empowered with the maximum number of choices and options?

What student performance indicators will be used to document that students have learned what they needed to know at a high enough level (mastery) to have the maximum number of choices and options?

The answers to these two questions provide the basis for backward mapping down through the other grades and subjects. For example, given the intended learning experiences identified for grade twelve, what prerequisite knowledge and skills do students need to master in grade eleven so that they are prepared for success at grade twelve? Through these conversations, it won't take long to specify what students need to learn at every grade level so they can be successful at the next.

In the context of a well thought-out curriculum that has been backward mapped, the teacher's role becomes clear: to prepare students so they can succeed at the next level of schooling. In a continuously improving system,

frequent monitoring of student progress is essential so that we can pinpoint the learning bottlenecks that cause teachers and students further down the line to invest time, effort, and energy in remedial work and relearning.

> *Most commonly, alignment of standards, assessment, and instruction is assumed if these components all address the same content topics. But this level of alignment is insufficient to assure that standards-based education will produce the desired results. . . . A more refined analysis is required that includes the depth of knowledge at which a topic is being addressed, the range of subtopics included, the balance among the subtopics, as well as how the topic advanced from grade to grade, and other criteria.*
>
> — The Center for the Study of Systemic Reform in Milwaukee Public Schools

What Evidence Should Be Used?

The beginning part of this chapter was designed to help you specify the intended curriculum of the district and school. The other two parts of the alignment discussion have to do with alignment between the intended curriculum and the assessed curriculum on the one hand and the intended curriculum and the taught curriculum on the other. We will now take up the alignment between the intended and assessed curriculum.

State mandated assessments must be considered fundamental to the overall

Backward Mapping

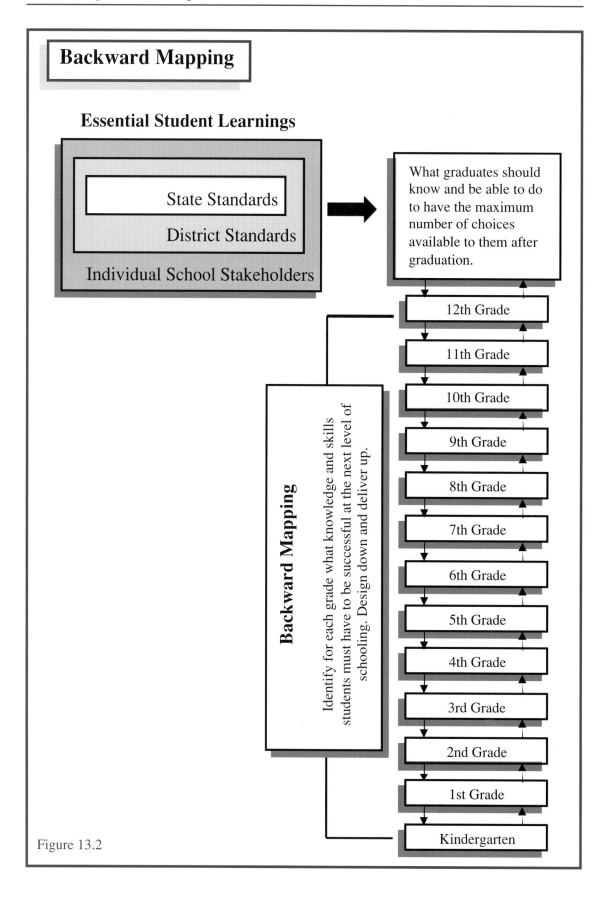

Figure 13.2

assessment system for the same reasons as the curricular standards described above. However, continuous improvement systems need more frequent information regarding student mastery of the essential curriculum than most state assessment programs require. Therefore, the school district must engage collaborative teams of teachers, administrators, and other stakeholders in developing an instructional management and assessment system that provides that needed information.

> *Alternative Measures. Some states give students alternative ways to demonstrate proficiency. For example, Wisconsin allows students to take either the MPS performance assessment or the Wisconsin Student Assessment System test. Researchers have found, however, that alternative measures create a critical alignment issue because their criteria can vary greatly from each other. It is possible for students to demonstrate proficiency on one and not the other because neither is fully aligned with the standards and both vary in the emphasis placed on topics.*
>
> — The Center for the Study of Systemic Reform in Milwaukee Public Schools.

This instructional management and assessment system must give students and teachers as near to real-time data as possible. The problem with much of the testing currently in place is that the feedback to students and their teachers is so delayed as to render it useless when it comes to improving student learning.

Most teachers have monitoring "tools" they use in their classrooms to make judgments about student learning and student performance. The use of available technology and some of the software management systems that are commercially available makes possible a just-in-time learning information system that can enable teachers to help students meet the performance standards.

One question that this conversation raises centers upon the frequency with which student progress should be monitored. The effective schools research and experience suggests that student progress should be monitored *as frequently as the teacher is prepared to adjust instruction*. If the teacher can adjust instruction everyday, monitor every day. If the teacher can only adjust instruction once a week, monitor once a week. However, if the teacher doesn't ever plan on adjusting instruction, why bother monitoring at all?

Alignment Between the Intended and Taught Curriculum

If we complete the process steps outlined above, we should be able to meet the standard of alignment between the intended and assessed curriculum. Whether the assessments are state-mandated, district-managed, or teacher-made, we should be able to determine whether the students are mastering the intended curriculum and meeting grade-level essential learnings.

Thus far, our process has prompted us to specify what we want students to know, do, and be disposed to do when

Outcomes Summary Worksheet

Subject Area

Sequence/level

Exit Outcome #

Learner Outcome

Assessment Criteria

Type of Assessment
- [ ] Portfolio
- [ ] Project Performance
- [ ] Observation
- [ ] Objective Test Type: _____ (e.g., SAT)

Related Learning Activities

Suggested Resources

Integrated Skill/Topic:

Access & Proc Info

Crit Think

Creativity

Life Skills

Interp Comm

Appl Tech

Career Opt

World Persp

Prin of Dem

Prin Econ Syst

Pers Eth Aesth

Domain:

Psychomotor

Cognitive

Affective

Figure 13.3

Outcomes Summary Completed Example

Subject Area

> Mathematics

Sequence/level

> Problem solving/
> 6th grade

Exit Outcome # 4

Integrated Skill/Topic:

Access & Proc Info	X
Crit Think	X
Creativity	X
Life Skills	X
Interp Comm	X
Appl Tech	X
Career Opt	
World Persp	
Prin of Dem	
Prin Econ Syst	
Pers Eth Aesth	

Learner Outcome

> Students will translate a written mathematical problem situation.

Assessment Criteria

> Teacher judgement of solution, student presentation.

Type of Assessment

[X] Portfolio   [X] Observation

[X] Project Performance   [ ] Objective Test

Type: _____ (e.g., SAT)

Domain:

Psychomotor	
Cognitive	X
Affective	

Related Learning Activities

> Group brainstorming, teacher modeling of problem solving techniques.

Suggested Resources

> Computers, texts, newspapers.

Figure 13.4

they finish school. From this understanding, we have backward mapped the curriculum so that we can benchmark the learner's progress toward these final goals all along the way. However, in the end, if the students are not taught the intended curriculum, all the previous work will have been for nothing.

> *The extent to which the taught curriculum matches the test items is crucial. According to one study, for example, found that curriculum alignment explained 72 percent of the variance in posttest reading scores.*
>
> — Wang, 1998

Obviously, the odds are much higher that students will learn those things they are taught than those they are not taught!

A Moral Mandate for Curriculum Alignment

Throughout this chapter we have addressed the issues around alignment from a practical point of view. We have spoken about the intentional nature of teaching and learning. We could have invoked old expressions like, "If you don't know where you're going, any road will get you there." These are very practical reasons to worry about the issues of alignment. We now turn to the moral issues surrounding alignment between curriculum, instruction, and assessment. That is, when a school ignores alignment issues, who pays the price for such negligence?

The first and most obvious answer would be the students. It is true that

students pay the highest price when adults ignore these critical issues. Even worse, those students who are most dependent on the school as their sole source of academic learning—poor and minority students—suffer even more when a school ignores alignment issues. How can the adults in a school or school district justify this situation—in effect, penalizing the students most in need—simply because the alignment issues have not been properly addressed?

The need for a tight alignment between the intended, taught, and tested curriculum extends beyond the needs of the students. If the alignment is not perceived to be present by *teachers*, the result will be increased levels of institutional and organizational anxiety. When anxiety levels among staff gets high enough, they may begin to behave in desperate and improper ways, from teaching in ways that are very inefficient and uninspiring to their students to out-and-out cheating.

Finally, when a school attempts to reform itself by changing programs, policies, and practices, how will it be able to assess whether the changes are making a difference unless the intended, taught, and assessed curricula are well aligned? Any innovation that is adopted by a school for the purpose of improving student learning and performance, by its very nature, presumes that there is good curriculum alignment. Anything else will result in wasted effort, wasted time, and wasted money in pursuit of change with no measurable, tangible benefit. In contrast, the process of alignment will yield significant increases in measured student performance for many schools and school districts.

Monitoring Curriculum, Assessment and Instructional Alignment

Continuous improvement educational systems are data-driven and depend heavily on timely feedback. In the context of curriculum, assessment, and instructional alignment, school districts must develop and implement feedback processes that allow the district to be assured that the students are actually being taught the intended curriculum. There two places where nonalignment is most likely to creep into the process: lesson planning and lesson delivery. To address these issues, districts should develop feedback systems to 1) assure that the lesson plans teachers develop are well aligned with the district's intended curriculum; and 2) assure that the intended curriculum was actually delivered in the classroom.

One of the best ways for the district to assure lesson plan alignment is to use technology to develop a lesson-planning template. The template should bring to the teacher's desk an aligned description of the grade-level and subject matter standards for which the teacher is accountable, while giving the teacher control over how the lesson is taught. Such an automated system would be a great tool for teachers and at the same time provide process data by which the district can monitor the alignment between the district's intended curriculum and the teacher's lesson plans.

The district also needs feedback data from every classroom in the district to be sure that the intended curriculum, reflected in teacher lesson plans, is actually taught to the students. Schools are complex systems and many times the lesson plan is not fully delivered. Sometimes the reasons for the slip between the intended and delivered curriculum are classroom specific and alterable by the individual teacher. Sometimes the slip between the intended and delivered curriculum is due to interruptions that are not under the control of the individual teacher or even individual school. Regardless of the cause, the effect on student learning is the same—a lost opportunity for students to learn what they need to know. These areas need to be identified, acknowledged, and addressed. This is an excellent example of a leading indicator for student learning based on the Effective Schools Correlate of Opportunity to Learn and Time on Task.

In a later section, we will address the issues of whether the students actually learned what they were taught. However, that analysis requires evidence that the students actually had the opportunity to learn the intended curriculum.

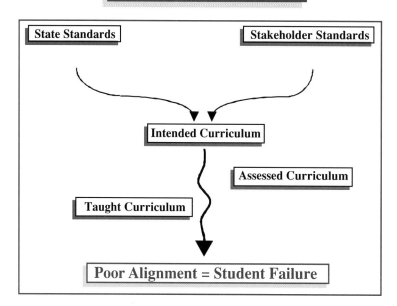

Curriculum Alignment

State Standards   Stakeholder Standards

Intended Curriculum

Assessed Curriculum

Taught Curriculum

Poor Alignment = Student Failure

State standards and stakeholder expectations merge like two tributaries of a river merging into the intended curriculum. When there is poor curriculum alignment, the assessed curriculum ends up on one bank and the taught curriculum on the other and our students end up "missing the boat."

When the curriculum is properly aligned, we all end up "in the same boat" headed for student success!

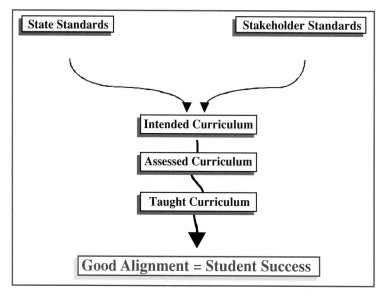

State Standards   Stakeholder Standards

Intended Curriculum

Assessed Curriculum

Taught Curriculum

Good Alignment = Student Success

Figure 13.5

KEY CONCEPTS

This chapter has focused on translating our vision of an educated person into a plan of action for schools and teachers.

- Begin with the end in mind: What should our children know and be able to do when they graduate? What skills and knowledge will give them the greatest range of choices?

- Design Down: given the goals outlined above, specify the skills and knowledge needed to successfully meet those goals. Work backward, specifying the skills needed in grade 11 to successfully navigate 12th grade, etc.

- Deliver Up: Children will learn what they are taught; make sure that the intended curriculum, the assessed curriculum, and the taught curriculum are aligned. This step in and of itself will no doubt result in higher student achievement.

Chapter 14

Study

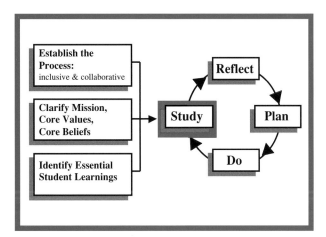

If we were not trying to improve an *existing* school, the first step in the continuous improvement process would be to develop a plan and then proceed to engage the other steps in the continuous improvement sequence. However, we are working to improve an operating school or district with a preexisting track record. Therefore, the first step, given the mission, is to ask, "How are we doing on our mission now?" If the mission is "learning for all," then the evidence that we must examine is the performance data that allows us to see who is learning and who is not.

The evidence that a school or district might use to assess mission attainment can be broad or narrow. For example, some schools may choose to examine only state assessment scores or other standardized test results because those represent the data for which they are held accountable. Other schools see these as a necessary but perhaps not sufficient array

of evidence to answer the question of how well the school or district is doing. In this case, the schools might augment test scores with other measures that they believe reflect some important aspect of the mission. For example, some schools monitor student performance on affective measures such as academic self-concept or student sense of efficacy. The continuous improvement process in no way demands more or less data than the school or district values. Furthermore, the continuous improvement process in no way limits the performance data that can or should be monitored. *What the continuous school improvement process does demand is that schools are explicit and intentional about what they plan to measure and monitor to judge mission accomplishment.*

To provide some guidance on the amount and types of evidence that should be examined, here are a few rules-of-thumb:

- **Strike a balance between too much and too little data.** On one hand, it's easier to keep the stakeholders focused when fewer rather than many sources of evidence are considered. On the other hand, to be credible with most of the stakeholder groups, enough data needs to be examined to satisfy their desire for the big picture. This decision is largely intuitive and the leadership team will need to be sensitive to stakeholder requests for more information.

- **Choose data sources that can be monitored over time.** Looking at evidence over time makes it easier to get a sense of trends and places less weight on any one data point. Often one point of evidence stands out because it is unusually good or bad. Multiple measures examined over time presents a more accurate picture of current reality in the school or district. In addition, the continuous improvement process requires us to examine the same sources of evidence after the

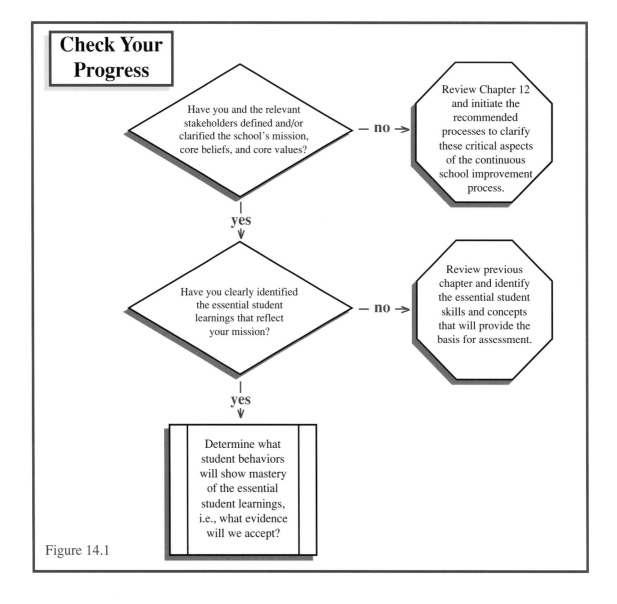

Check Your Progress

Have you and the relevant stakeholders defined and/or clarified the school's mission, core beliefs, and core values?

— no → Review Chapter 12 and initiate the recommended processes to clarify these critical aspects of the continuous school improvement process.

yes

Have you clearly identified the essential student learnings that reflect your mission?

— no → Review previous chapter and identify the essential student skills and concepts that will provide the basis for assessment.

yes

Determine what student behaviors will show mastery of the essential student learnings, i.e., what evidence will we accept?

Figure 14.1

planned changes have been implemented to give us an accurate picture of the results.

- **Choose data that is aligned with clearly identified essential learner outcomes.** In the previous chapter, you worked at clarifying the mission and identifying essential learner outcomes. It is critical that the data you collect are aligned with these outcomes or you will be missing the mark when evaluating how well you are achieving your mission.

Curriculum Mastery

As we mentioned in Chapter 9, the Effective Schools Framework has historically emphasized the concept of **curriculum mastery** when evaluating progress on the mission of "learning for all." Curriculum mastery is defined as *the level of achievement that students must reach to be predictably successful at the next level of schooling.* Mastery standards can be empirically determined by examining trend data of past student performance. For example, you may have determined that curricular mastery for 5th grade mathematics (that is, what standard a fifth-grader has to meet to be successful in 6th grade math) includes one or more of the following:

- Attain 75 percent mastery on all teacher-made math tests.

- Score in the 5th stanine (40th percentile) on the math section of the SAT.

- Obtain letter grade of C or above in math at the end of each marking period.

Two kinds of student outcome data may be collected as the yardstick for measuring progress on the mission: student achievement data and student affective data. The following list, although not exhaustive by any means, gives you some specific examples of achievement and affective data.

Student Achievement Data

- Tests
  - Standardized, norm-referenced
  - Standardized, criterion-referenced
  - Teacher-developed

- Other Academic Measures
  - Letter grade distribution
  - Retention percentage, by grade level
  - Grade point average, by subject and grade level
  - Student course selection (e.g., AP classes), by grade level

---

Student Affective Data

- Student conduct reports

- Student attendance

- Participation in extracurricular activities

- Student awards

- Homework completion rates

- Opinion surveys

- Checklists and observations

Putting It All Together: Linking the Mission, Essential Student Learnings, and Data Collection

Mission Statement

Essential Student Learnings

I. _____

II. _____

etc. _____

Essential Student Learning I. _____

_____

Evidence of Attainment:

Evidence Available	Evidence Needed
1.	1.
2.	2.
3.	3.
4.	4.

Figure 14.2

Data Analysis

Because this Continuous School Improvement Model is based on the Effective Schools research, it is concerned with both the quality and equity of the education that students experience. Therefore, we need to examine the evidence in a way that will permit the leadership team to answer questions regarding both quality and equity of the school's instructional program. When collecting and analyzing the data at the macro level, that is for the entire student population, the level of achievement to which the entire group rises reflects the quality dimension of the school. The distribution of that achievement across major subsets of the student population reflects the equity dimension. The process of analyzing the data for these distinct subgroups is called **disaggregation of the data.** The topic of data disaggregation is covered in depth in Chapter 9—Data Analysis Tools. Here we will simply review some key points and relate them to our current discussion of data analysis.

Disaggregating the data requires that you determine the number and percent of students in specified groupings [e.g., gender, racial or ethnic, or socioeconomic status (SES)] that meet or exceed the identified curricular mastery standards. Only then can the school leadership team determine where there are discrepancies between the mission and the results the school is currently getting. You may find that your school does not have any gap among groups in mastering one content area, but may have a significant gap in another content area. Or you may find no gender gap in the percentage of students demonstrating mastery, but may find significant gaps when students from differing racial/ethnic groups or SES groupings are compared. It would be rare indeed where a school would have all students attaining curricular mastery with no gaps in the percentage of the various groups who are evidencing success. Clearly, that is our goal *as long as the overall quality indicators are also high*. This means that, even if there are no achievement gaps among subgroups, there is no reason to celebrate if everyone is doing poorly.

As suggested previously, whenever possible more than one data point (e.g., test scores plus writing samples plus observation) should be examined. Multiple measures taken at about the same time provide the leadership team with more confidence in their conclusions. Likewise, looking at the same or similar data over time (e.g., state test scores for the past three years) allows the leadership team to get a clearer picture of the school's achievement trends. Approaching the data in this way will give the team a sense as to whether the problems with quality or equity are getting better, worse, or remaining relatively stable.

Often educators new to the process of disaggregating student performance data are disappointed with the tool because it doesn't provide any clues as to how the school can or should go about solving the observed achievement level or gap problems. We stress once more that disaggregating student achievement data is **not** a problem-*solving* strategy; it is a problem-*finding* strategy. Nevertheless, the power of the process can not be

Data Analysis: Disaggregating the Data

Math scores disaggregated by gender.

Raw Data

Number	Sex	Math	Number	Sex	Math	Number	Sex	Math
1	F	77	11	F	92	21	F	79
2	M	89	12	M	75	22	M	97
3	F	74	13	M	70	23	M	85
4	F	68	14	M	95	24	F	84
5	M	65	15	F	67	25	F	86
6	M	86	16	M	89	26	F	76
7	F	63	17	M	58	27	F	73
8	M	55	18	M	81	28	M	98
9	M	50	19	F	89	29	F	98
10	M	78	20	M	91	30	M	93

Charted Data

	Female	**Male**
80 and Above	Number= 5 Percent = 38%	Number= 10 Percent = 59%
79 and Below	Number= 8 Percent = 62%	Number= 7 Percent = 41%
	TOTAL= 13	TOTAL= 17

Graphed Data

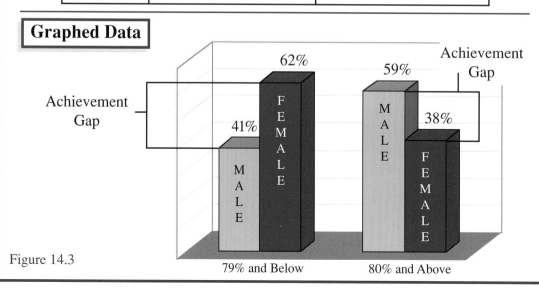

Figure 14.3

overstated since every problem-solving model starts with an accurate description of the problem.

Getting To Root Causes

One of the first functions of a leader or leadership group is to accurately frame the problem to be solved. The school leadership team frames the problem based on the in-depth analysis of the chosen data. The discrepancies that were identified between the stated mission and data will then become the focus of school improvement.

Once the leadership team frames the problem based on an analysis of the data—that is, they have identified and defined the discrepancy between the school's mission of "learning for all" and the observed achievement data—the question now turns to **why** we have these observed discrepancies. This will require the leadership team to engage in another process called root cause analysis. As we describe in Chapter 8, some have referred to this process as the *5 Whys*. This process is critical to the continuous school improvement process because—as you will recall from the chapter on Systems Theory—our existing mental models may cause us to jump to the wrong conclusion as to why a problem exists and, in turn, apply the wrong solution. Not only may this not solve the identified problem, it may in fact exacerbate it, or create another related

Steps to Get to the Root Causes

1. Examine your school's most recent State test results.

2. Pay specific attention to variability in the student scores.

3. Brainstorm why you believe the bottom 1/3 performed so poorly.

4. For each hypothesis, describe what data you currently have or could collect to determine whether the hypothesis is true or not.

5. Develop an action plan with appropriate timelines to collect and analyze these data.

6. For each valid hypothesis, brainstorm as to why the valid hypothesis is true.

Figure 14.4

Getting to Root Causes Worksheet

Step 1 Focus on the students who scored in the bottom 1/3 on your school's State test results. What is your hypothesis as to why they performed as poorly as they did?

1. Hypothesis I:

   _____

2. Hypothesis II:

   _____

3. Hypothesis III:

   _____

4. Hypothesis IV:

   _____

5. Hypothesis V:

   _____

Step 2 For each hypothesis, list current or new data that could be collected and analyzed to provide evidence for the hypothesis.

1. Hypothesis I   Evidence: _____

   Action Plan & Timeline: _____

2. Hypothesis II   Evidence: _____

   Action Plan & Timeline: _____

3. Hypothesis III   Evidence: _____

   Action Plan & Timeline: _____

4. Hypothesis IV   Evidence: _____

   Action Plan & Timeline: _____

5. Hypothesis V   Evidence: _____

   Action Plan & Timeline: _____

Figure 14.5

problem. The 5 Whys process encourages us to "drill down" beyond the obvious and superficial and find the ultimate or "root" cause of a particular problem.

The Four "Common Places" of Education

In a 1962 paper, educational philosopher and scholar Joseph J. Schwab described the four common places of education. He stated that a complete thought in education requires some reference to someone (usually a teacher), teaching someone (the learner), something (curriculum), in some setting (usually the classroom). This framework has proven to be useful in pursuing the root causes for achievement problems in schools.

The Four Common Places framework helps us organize our thinking when trying to determine the root causes of the identified gaps: Does the problem reside in the learners and the learning processes used? Does the problem reside in the teacher and the teaching processes used? Does the

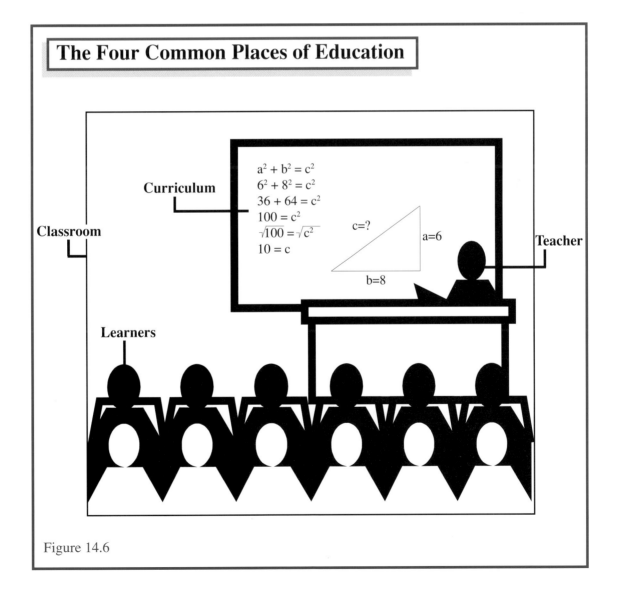

Figure 14.6

problem reside in the content or subject matter to be learned? Or, does the problems reside in the context or setting in which the learning was to occur?

Taking this one step further, the root causes of the achievement problems in a school could reside in more than one of the four common places, even in all four common places. Furthermore, the problem may derive from interactions among the four common places. For example, maybe certain student learning styles don't work well with certain teaching styles. We need to pursue the root causes of our achievement problem by initially "casting a wide net" for the potential causes and then letting the data we gather help us to rule out one or more of the common places or their interactions.

The first theories of cause to be gathered should come from the stakeholders—especially those working closest to the point where the learning mission meets the road, in the classroom. The rules that guide the process are simple and should be rigorously implemented.

- Members of the stakeholder group can suggest as many different hypotheses as to the root cause of the achievement problem as they feel are valid.

- All of the stakeholder hypotheses will be taken seriously if, and only if, they can be corroborated with data.

- The data can be based on information that is already a part of the archive of the school (e. g.,

attendance) or data that could be collected if the leadership team and stakeholders form a plan for its collection and analysis.

- Theories-of-cause will not remain in the potentially valid category if no data exist and no data can be collected to support them.

The concept of the *5 Whys* or going to root causes is designed to keep going deeper and deeper until one gets to the "rock bottom" cause of the problem. The process is powerful and will take time to complete since the number of theories of the problem maybe large and you will either accept or refute a suggested cause by examining data on an item-by-item basis. You will find links to the problem you are researching that seem logical and obvious. However, to assure that you have found the *root cause*, you should continue to "drill down" beyond the obvious by asking "Why?" Getting to the rock bottom cause of a problem is the only way to assure that the problem, once solved, will stay solved.

Once a list of root causes has been identified and those not supported by data eliminated, the leadership team can begin a process of prioritizing the valid list of causes to address. Two strategies may be used to set priorities. First, the leadership team may prioritize the list based on those that have the broadest support from the stakeholder groups. Second, and arguably the most important way for the leadership team to prioritize the list, is to base it on the probable impact each has on the learning and performance of the students. For example, if students are learning what they are being taught but the curriculum is not aligned with the assessments, alignment would have a direct and immediate impact on student learning and student performance. On the other hand, improving the communication skills of the principal may be a valuable change in a school, but would not likely have much of a direct or immediate effect on student learning and performance. This example shows the difference between a "results-driven" intervention and an "activities-driven" intervention. Clearly, as the labels imply, results-driven interventions are likely to have the most direct and immediate impact on student learning and student performance.

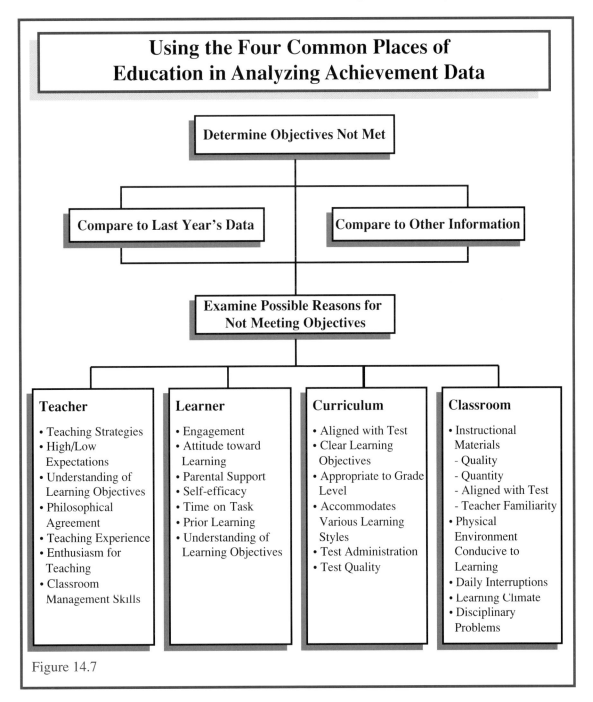

Using the Four Common Places of Education in Analyzing Achievement Data

Determine Objectives Not Met

Compare to Last Year's Data **Compare to Other Information**

Examine Possible Reasons for Not Meeting Objectives

Teacher
- Teaching Strategies
- High/Low Expectations
- Understanding of Learning Objectives
- Philosophical Agreement
- Teaching Experience
- Enthusiasm for Teaching
- Classroom Management Skills

Learner
- Engagement
- Attitude toward Learning
- Parental Support
- Self-efficacy
- Time on Task
- Prior Learning
- Understanding of Learning Objectives

Curriculum
- Aligned with Test
- Clear Learning Objectives
- Appropriate to Grade Level
- Accommodates Various Learning Styles
- Test Administration
- Test Quality

Classroom
- Instructional Materials
  - Quality
  - Quantity
  - Aligned with Test
  - Teacher Familiarity
- Physical Environment Conducive to Learning
- Daily Interruptions
- Learning Climate
- Disciplinary Problems

Figure 14.7

Sample Survey

XYZ High School Staff Survey

Demographic Information

1. Gender
    ❏ Female (girl)   ❏ Male (boy)

2. Race/Ethnicity
    ❏ White   ❏ African-American   ❏ Hispanic/Latino
    ❏ Native American   ❏ Asian   ❏ Other Races

> SA = Strongly Agree
> A = Agree
> U = Undecided
> D = Disagree
> SD = Strongly Disagree
> NA = Not Applicable or No Opinion

Safe & Orderly Environment	SA	A	U	D	SD	NA
3. Dealing with discipline problems in my class uses up a lot of instructional time.	❏	❏	❏	❏	❏	❏

High Expectations for Success						
4. Our school staff communicates the belief that all children can learn.	❏	❏	❏	❏	❏	❏

Instructional Leadership						
5. The principal has established a strong academic focus in the school.	❏	❏	❏	❏	❏	❏

Home-School Relations						
6. There is a weak parent participation and support of the school's programs.	❏	❏	❏	❏	❏	❏

Clear & Focused Mission						
7. I don't understand the overall purpose and priorities of the school.	❏	❏	❏	❏	❏	❏

Opportunity to Learn/Time on Task						
8. All necessary supplies and materials for basic skills instruction are available.	❏	❏	❏	❏	❏	❏

Frequent Monitoring of Student Progress						
9. I think standardized tests provide useful information about student achievement.	❏	❏	❏	❏	❏	❏

Survey questions taken from Reality Check[SM]. More information on this tool is available in the appendix.

Figure 14.8

Needs Assessment Survey Data

A second strategy for getting to the causes of poor performance is to conduct a needs assessment survey. Needs assessment tools are based upon respondent perceptions of the current status of the school or district. With individual perceptions, there are no right or wrong answers; therefore, respondents are not expected or required to defend their perceptions with any supportive data. Although needs assessments yield subjective data—as opposed to test scores, which are objective measures—we should not underestimate the significance of stakeholder perceptual data. We need to be reminded of the sociological axiom that says that if something is perceived as real, it becomes real in its consequences.

Needs assessments, by their very nature, are developed out of a theory or framework of cause and effect. That is to say, when we develop a series of questions to ask our stakeholders, we create those questions from a theory of cause and effect. Throughout this book, we have been building a model of continuous school improvement that integrates the Effective Schools framework with the theories of Continuous Improvement and Systems Thinking. In an earlier chapter, we discussed the Correlates of Effective Schools as our cause/effect framework to help inform the problems in the school. In this chapter, we use that conceptual framework as the basis from which to solicit stakeholder perceptions of the presence or absence, strength or weakness of each of the Correlates in their school.

Conducting surveys as a way of studying the problems of a school or district can play a valuable role in framing the problems. Survey research is a complex process and members of the leadership team must become generally familiar with the "rules of the game." The survey process has been discussed earlier in this book. In addition to that information, there are many books and supportive materials available that will ensure that we use the survey technology properly. This chapter will not go into more detail regarding survey methodology, but such study is strongly recommended.

Stakeholder perceptions should change as a school intervenes to change policies, practices, and procedures designed to improve student learning and student performance. Surveys must be readministered from time to time to determine whether the interventions are having the desired positive impact. For example, if the stakeholders perceived a problem with discipline and the school adopts a policy of school uniforms, it will be important to see whether the perceived discipline problem has improved. It would also be important to assess whether there were other unintended consequences, whether positive or negative.

Leading Indicator Data Analysis

Throughout this book, continuous school improvement has focused on measured student achievement and other results-oriented data to assess progress on the school's mission. As central and significant as these measures are, they are of limited value in the improvement process itself. As was noted earlier, disaggregated student achievement data is a problem-finding strategy, not a problem-solving strategy. The 5 Whys and the needs assessment survey tools help the leadership team focus on finding the root causes of the achievement problems highlighted by the earlier analyses. The third strategy builds on the concepts of leading and trailing indicators.

The Leading and Trailing Indicators Revisited

As we noted in Chapter 2, the reason why the analysis of measured student achievement is of limited value as a problem-solving process is because it is an after-the-fact measure of student learning. It trails behind the student's learning much like the little red wagon trails behind the little boy pulling it down the street. The continuous improvement scholars have long recognized the limitations of looking at results in hopes of improving the processes that produced the results. Even though the various accountability systems have virtually everyone— parents, teachers, and politicians— staring at test scores, they will not inform the improvement needs directly. What are schools to do?

Schools committed to continuous school improvement must monitor and assess the **leading indicators of learning** and make changes in those where necessary. Appropriate changes in the leading indicators of learning will, by definition, result in changes in learning and, subsequently, measured student achievement. Perhaps the easiest way to illustrate the logic of the concept is with a negative example. Does anyone doubt that if a teacher significantly reduces the time spent teaching students the content needed to master grade level standards, that learning and achievement is likely to go down?

Unfortunately, most schools in the United States today do **not** monitor and assess any leading indicators of learning on a systematic and regular basis. Before schools are truly going to benefit from the theory and practices of continuous school improvement, they must install data-gathering systems that will provide, on an ongoing basis, information on the leading indicators of learning. One may wonder how schools could exist for this many years and not have existing systems that provide these important indicators.

There are two interrelated answers to this question. First, until quite recently, school learning was optional; therefore, measuring and monitoring the variables that cause learning were also optional. When the mission of public education was changed by the accountability movement to "learning for all," the need for leading indicators of learning became apparent to many almost immediately. Second, until the mission changed, schools operated teacher-centered instructional systems. Now, because of the new mission, schools must adopt a learning-centered instructional system. Once the commitment to developing and maintaining a continuously improving learning-centered system is made, the need to monitor and analyze data focused on learning becomes clear.

Where should school leadership teams turn to find guidance in selecting a leading indicator system? There are two interrelated bodies of research that can and should serve as the basis for a leading indicator system. The first comes from the Effective Schools Research and centers around the Correlates of Effective Schools. The second comes from the knowledge base provided by the research on human learning. Learning-centered systems would obviously use knowledge of human learning to guide and inform school practices. Such has not been the case in teacher-centered systems.

Effective Schools Correlates as Leading Indicators of Learning

In the following section, each of the Correlates of Effective Schools will be listed and one or two indicator variables for each will be presented. Schools serious about the process of continuous school improvement will develop monitoring systems that will help to truly change those school and classroom dimensions that affect learning and subsequent achievement.

Safe and Orderly Environment

A leading classroom-level indicator of a safe and orderly environment would monitor, on a daily or weekly basis, the number of times where classroom instruction had been interrupted for more than two or three minutes because of discipline problems. All classroom interruptions are a concern because they steal time from learning. Lost time due to disciplinary problems is a serious concern for two reasons. First, students who are involved directly in such incidents are obviously not on task and they are not learning. Second, these incidents curtail the capacity of the other students to maintain their focus on learning. Classrooms with more discipline problems, other things being equal, are going to have less learning and reduced achievement.

Another indicator has to do with those more severe disciplinary incidents where students become "repeat offenders." To the extent that this is true, whatever classroom management strategy the teacher uses isn't working for these students. Clearly, the teacher needs help in finding different and more effective strategies.

Clear and Focused Mission

Previously we addressed the issue of operationalizing the "learning for all" mission by developing an aligned curriculum that is associated with clear grade-level standards or essential learnings. One possible leading indicator of learning would be to monitor, on either a daily or weekly basis, which standards or essential learnings were the focus of instruction and how much time was actually allocated to these standards. The theory being advanced around this leading indicator says that if teachers don't make a conscious and deliberate effort to teach the standards, students—especially the disadvantaged—won't learn them.

Second, teacher-centered systems focus on the amount of time allocated for the teaching of a concept or lesson. Learning-centered systems need to focus not only on the amount of time spent on teaching, but on what additional time was needed for practice to assure learning.

Opportunity to Learn, Time on Task

One of the most important leading indicators of learning centers on the amount of time students are authentically engaged in the work of learning. Teachers won't need to obsess over accountability and test scores if two conditions exist:

- There is tight alignment between the intended, taught, and tested curriculum, **and**

- all students spend the necessary time actively engaged in the work of learning.

The hypothesis being advanced around this indicator is that engagement—or maybe more accurately, non-engagement—is an early indicator of less learning and ultimately lower measured performance.

As a leading indicator of learning, time on task can be defined more generally or fairly precisely. If one were to observe a group of students in a classroom, most observers with minimal training could agree which students were engaged in the work of learning and which were not. This is an example of a general definition. A much more precise indicator of student engagement has to do with the concept of the **zone of proximal development** and learning prerequisites. The zone of proximal development is defined as the relative distance the new learning can be from prior learning before the learner can and will be able to successfully learn the new material.

Students can be outside their zone of proximal development in two ways. First, the student may have already mastered the current content and is therefore not challenged and may be even bored. Such a student could be described as being off-task and as being denied an opportunity to learn. The second way—one that seems much more prevalent, especially for the disadvantaged—is that the student lacks the necessary prerequisites for the new learning. Such students could also be described as off-task and being denied an opportunity to learn.

Obviously, our goal would be to have all students in their respective zone all the time. This goal is virtually unattainable in a teacher-centered system that places students on the basis of chronological age and gives each student the same amount of time to learn. The learning-centered system, in contrast, will customize learning to each student according to need.

High Expectations for Success

Expectations are defined as internal beliefs that teachers hold in their hearts regarding their students' success. The research literature is clear on two points regarding teacher expectations for student success. First, teachers form their expectations early in the school year. Second, once formed, teacher expectations for student success become relatively firm and tend to function as a self-fulfilling prophecy.

In an attempt to prevent or reduce the self-fulfilling nature of teacher expectations, a leading indicator of this correlate should be monitored on a daily or weekly basis. Teachers should be asked to indicate student-by-student which student did or did not meet the their expectations today or this week. Student performance may depart from the teacher expectations in two ways. First, student work could exceed the teacher's expectations for that task or assignment. In this case, the teacher would be pleasantly surprised and should acknowledge this fact to the student and adjust the expectations for future performance upward.

Alternately, the student's work may fall below the teacher's expectations. Obviously, the teacher would be disappointed and may be tempted to acknowledge this to the student and lower expectations for that student's future performance (no one likes being proven wrong). However, lowering expectations is not a useful strategy because it moves us away from the "learning for all" mission, not toward it. In fact, lowering expectations usually starts a downward spiral of lower expectations leading to less effort and poorer performance, resulting in still lower expectations.

In both cases where teacher expectations are found to be inaccurate, the question of "why" needs to be explored. When student achievement is above or below expectation, the teacher can learn a great deal by exploring the reasons for the incongruity between expectation and performance.

Expectations are powerful leading indicators of learning. Sometimes the only source of energy the learner can summon to a task is the energy that comes when a significant other, like a teacher, believes that they can succeed.

Frequent Monitoring of Student Progress

Testing is but one part of the monitoring processes associated with this leading indicator. For purposes of discussion, we will define monitoring as *any review of student work that is accompanied by timely corrective feedback*. Monitoring may be based on oral responses, written assignments, teacher-made tests, teacher observations of performances, and so forth.

Paradoxically, most formal tests that students are required to take—such as standardized norm-referenced tests or state-mandated standards-based tests—do not qualify as monitoring student progress at all. To qualify as monitoring, *the test must be followed with timely corrective feedback and knowledge of results*. Many formal assessments fail to provide students with corrective feedback in a timely fashion. As a result, they are of little value as tools for frequently monitoring student progress so we can adjust instruction to facilitate learning.

On more than one occasion, we have recommended less "testing" and more "monitoring." How frequently teachers should monitor student progress depends on how often they are prepared to adjust instruction to meet the diverse learning needs of their students. As we have said before, the only purpose for monitoring without adjusting instruction is to select and sort students.

The questions teachers may be expected to respond to regarding this correlate proceed in two directions. Some address the frequency of teacher monitoring; others ask for feedback regarding the instructional adjustments that were made as a result of that monitoring. Here are examples:

- During the past week, how many times was student mastery of a part of the intended curriculum formally monitored (using tests, project reports, or home work)? Was corrective feedback given? Were the results incorporated into the teacher's record book?

- Based on the formal monitoring of student performance, how many times did the teacher adjust subsequent instruction? What type of adjustments did the teacher make? Were these adjustments sufficient to assure that all the students in the learning group mastered the intended curriculum objective?

- If report cards were distributed today, which students, if any, would receive a grade indicating less than satisfactory progress in mastering the essential learnings as specified in the curricula?

The more frequent the monitoring, the more precise the feedback. The faster the feedback is delivered, the more monitoring contributes to improved learning by helping to build a just-in-time information and intervention system. You will recall this concept from Chapter 3:

> In a just-in-time intervention system, help comes immediately and in sufficient quantity and quality to effectively and efficiently assist the learner in meeting the instructional object.

This system requires the frequent monitoring of key work processes, followed by corrective feedback and knowledge-based adjustments in those processes. Frequent monitoring of student progress, as a leading indicator, is intended to provide the teacher with the type of information needed to make changes in the teaching/learning situation as quickly as possible. Some instructional adjustments will be made for a single student, some for small-groups, and still others for the entire class.

If we can assume that the teacher is well grounded in the research and proven practices associated with human learning, we can expect that the adjustments the teacher makes for individual students or the group as whole are well thought out and likely to prove effective. Only adequate and ongoing training, professional development, and reflective and collaborative learning and practice will ensure that teachers are equipped to effectively monitor and adjust.

Positive Home/School Relations

Whenever teachers are asked to indicate what variable they believe could have the greatest positive impact on student achievement, they answer "the parents." The overwhelming majority of teachers say that student learning is most successful when a partnership exists between teacher and parents. Unfortunately, most teacher preparation programs offer little, if any, training to prospective teachers in how to best establish and maintain such partnerships. As a result, parent visits, parent conferences, and even telephone conversations represent a source of anxiety for many teachers.

Recent changes in Federal Title I legislation have begun to formally recognize the importance of the home-school partnership. Title I schoolwide project schools are now required to develop a parent compact in which mutual expectations and reciprocal accountability are set out. In some ways, this well-intended effort attempts to solve the problem from the wrong end. Teachers need training and support on how to deal with a wide variety of parenting styles. In addition, the leadership must be prepared to support the teachers in their efforts to make such partnerships work on behalf of all students.

In the continuous school improvement system, the home-school relations correlate would be continuously monitored through the following questions:

- Were there teacher-initiated parent/ teacher conferences this week for the primary purpose of giving the parents good news about their child's achievement? If yes, which parents were contacted?

- Were there teacher-initiated parent/ teacher conferences this week for the primary purpose of giving the parents bad news about their child's achievement? If yes, which parents were contacted?

- Were there parent-initiated parent/ teacher conferences this week? If yes, which parents were involved?

- How many specific requests did the teacher make in which parents were asked to provide explicit assistance to their child on school-related work?

- Does recent evidence suggest that some parents cannot be counted upon to help their children in response to specific teacher requests?

Our model of the continuous school improvement system is based on the belief that all children can and will learn, regardless of the home and family background of the child. In the ideal world, parents and the teacher should be in a close and caring partnership on behalf of the child's learning. Clearly, it is much easier to assure high levels of learning if this were the case. However, the absence of such a partnership does not mean that the child cannot or would not be expected to learn. On the contrary, if the data indicates a problem, some differentiated or customized alternative is needed. For example, when a parent is inaccessible—either through disinterest or circumstances—some sort of academic foster parent program, such as senior citizen mentors will help fulfill the student's need for help and support.

Strong Instructional Leadership

The correlate of strong instructional leadership has been saved for last, but not because it is less important. Rather, this correlate changes the framework for collecting and monitoring data from the individual classroom to the school as a whole.

Two important caveats are worth noting. First, as the frontline workers with the students, teachers have the most direct and immediate impact on learning and, in that sense, deserve to be placed first in this discussion. Second, the impact that the leadership has relative to achieving the mission will be mediated through the teachers and the learning groups. Therefore, the focus of this correlate will be on the administrative behaviors that guide, support, and monitor the teacher's efforts to deliver "learning for all." Each administrator will be expected to complete a continuous improvement progress report; if two or more administrators are involved, their data will be aggregated to form an overall administrative leadership profile.

In reflecting on the description of strong instructional leadership, it should be clear that the leader has a pervasive responsibility for making sure that everyone understands the mission and core values of the school.

The noted management guru and author, Tom Peters, said that big organizations, by virtue of their "bigness," are always subject to drift from the mission and core values. He defined a big organization as any organization that includes more than **four people**! Clearly, most schools include more than four people and therefore are subject to drift from the mission and core

values. The first obligation of the principal is to prevent the drift from occurring. A popular expression that sums up this important leadership function states that, "The main thing is to keep the main thing the main thing."

How should the principal strive to prevent this seemingly inevitable drift? Proactively, the principal needs to seize on every chance that comes along to remind teachers, parents, support staff, and students themselves of the school's mission. This constant message sets high expectations and controls the discourse in the learning environment.

Interactively, the leader needs to invest as much time and energy as is realistically possible in the place where the mission of learning meets the road— in the classrooms. The focus of these visits should be to monitor and support student mastery of the essential curriculum.

Reactively, the principal needs to focus as much of the organizational energy as is feasible on the data that indicate the extent to which the school is achieving its mission.

The leader must continually reinforce the belief that all children can and will learn. The principal must accept responsibility for assuring that every teacher has the knowledge and skills necessary to deliver the mission. The principal, on behalf of the entire school system, must empower teachers to act on behalf of the mission. How the individual leader chooses to develop these three domains can be a matter of personal preference and style. The only requirement is some positive action in each domain on an ongoing basis.

To capture the appropriate data about the leader's behavior, two types of data should be monitored: the number of different incidents of the expected behaviors and the amount of time devoted to each. The following are examples of the type of information needed from each administrator:

- This past week, were you involved in a disciplinary problem that was referred by a teacher? If so, how many and how much time was devoted to these problems?

- This past week, were you involved in a disciplinary problem that came to your attention from someone other than a teacher (or you observed it yourself)? How many such incidents occurred and how much time was devoted to these problems?

- Were you involved in administrator-initiated parent/teacher conferences this past week? If so, how many and how much time was devoted?

- Were other administrators involved in any parent/teacher conferences initiated by either the teacher or the parent? If so, how many and how much time was devoted to them?

- Have you discussed the expectations, mission, and core values of the system with parents, teachers in a group setting, students, or others? If so, to whom and how many times?

- How many classroom visits did you make during this past week and how much time was devoted to each?

- How much time did you spend, either alone or with others, studying the school's leading indicator data? What actions, if any, were taken as a result of examining the continuous progress data?

- What other activities occupied your time and energy this past week? Can some of those be eliminated or delegated to free more time for leading the mission and instructional elements in the system?

It is critical that the administrators and teachers understand that no one is suggesting that they aren't extremely busy and constantly working hard. In the case of the teacher, the question is how much of the time and effort is directed to the essential curriculum? In the case of the administrators, the question is how much time and energy was focused on the mission-critical activities and the instructional priorities of the system?

One of the goals of the leading indicator system is to document those activities that command time and attention, but are not tightly aligned with the learning mission of the system. Many of these activities cannot be avoided, but if some could be modified or eliminated, and that time and energy redirected to the core purpose of the system, student achievement would increase.

Putting It All Together:
Using the Data to Define a Learning Problem

Below is an example of how disaggregated student achievement data and correlate assessment data can be combined to create a clear description of a learning problem.

Student Achievement Data

• Over the past three academic years, 46% of boys in grades 2, 3, 4, and 5 received less than a "C" grade in reading on their report cards. This compares to 22% of girls receiving less than a "C."

• Over the past three academic years, an average of 28% of fourth-grade boys have achieved "proficient" status on the reading portion of the state standardized test. This compares with an average of 56% of fourth-grade girls achieving "proficient" status over the same period of time.

• Analysis of the state standardized test results indicates that fourth-grade boys are performing less well than girls in two specific reading areas: identifying story elements and using reading strategies to construct meaning.

Correlate Assessment Data

• 59% of staff rate student enthusiasm for learning as "low" or "very low."

• 63% of staff rate daily interruptions in learning as "high" or "very high."

• 10% of staff see little overlap between state standardized tests and course content.

• 27% of staff feel accountable for student achievement.

• 76% of staff find class management "difficult" or "very difficult."

Problem Statement

Over the past three years, boy have not mastered the essential learnings for reading. When compared to their female peers, evidence indicates that an average of 46% of boys in grades 2 to 5 received less than a "C" on their report cards, while only 22% of girls received similar grades. In addition, an average of 28% of fourth-grade boys have achieved "proficient" status on the mathematics portion of the state standardized test, while 56% of girls attained that status.

Figure 14.9

Putting It All Together:
Using the Data to Define a Learning Problem (continued)

Finding the Root Causes: Why might this problem exist?	Using the Data: Substantiating our "hunches."
Learner: Boys are absent more than girls and frequent absences cause gaps in learning.	Data show that boys on average miss 2-3 days more school per marking period than girls. Boys who are not achieving mastery in reading are absent more than 8 days per marking period.
Curriculum: The reading curriculum does not include topics of interest to boys.	**Data Needs:** review reading texts; correlate assessment of Opportunity to Learn/Time on Task: assess student engagement of boys vs. girls by observation or survey.
Teacher: Teachers have lower expectations of boys' ability in reading.	Factors affecting teacher expectations: 59% of staff rate student enthusiasm for learning "low" or "very low." In addition, 76% of staff find class management "difficult" or "very difficult." **Data Needs:** correlate assessment of students' performance compared to teacher expectations disaggregated by gender.
Classroom: There are too many distractions and interruptions during the day and boys have more trouble staying or getting back on task.	The correlate assessment data show that 63% of staff rate daily interruptions in learning as "high" or "very high." In addition, 76% of staff find class management "difficult" or "very difficult."

The above chart shows only the first level of Root Cause Analysis. The leadership team would then continue to ask WHY until the causes of the achievement gap in reading between boys and girls are identified with as much certainty as the data supports. You are then ready to move on to the second step in the Continuous School Improvement Process: **REFLECTION**

Figure 14.9

KEY CONCEPTS

- The primary aim of the first step in the continuous improvement system, **study**, is to frame the problem or problems of the school given the school's mission and core values using a variety of specific data.

- The specific types of information that were recommended for collection and analysis were not exhaustive. If other types of data are deemed to be meaningful and informative, by all means, incorporate them in the data-gathering procedures.

- In the continuous improvement system, collecting data on a one-time basis is usually not very helpful. Plans need to be made to collect the same type of data over to determine whether the action plans that are implemented are achieving their desired goal.

- Data-gathering should be developed as an ongoing *system*. Procedures for capturing the information in a timely and efficient manner must be given careful consideration at the outset.

- Gathering more and more information is always a temptation in the early stages of a continuous improvement process. Be careful not to get bogged-down in the "paralysis of analysis."

- It is better to focus on a few vital data points and follow the path they reveal, than to gather too much data and end up overwhelmed.

- Trailing indicators do not tell us **how** to improve. Leading indicators based on the Correlates of Effective Schools allow us to influence the factors that impact learning.

Chapter 15

Reflect

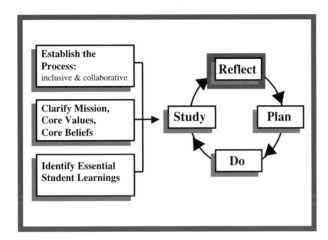

Reflection seems an appropriate title for this chapter because we are going to be asking the school improvement team and others to "ponder" or "consider" the identified problems and what might be done to successfully address it. Although this "ritual of reflection" is described as if it is a separate and distinct process, it really is something that is done throughout the continuous school improvement process. During the study stage discussed in the previous chapter, we described a reflection process about the data itself, looking for the root causes of the problems we identified through analysis of the data. The process of collecting, analyzing, and reflecting upon the data, the problems it highlights, and the root causes it identifies can be considered an **internal scanning process**. Now we turn to a broader use of the reflection process that will bring in outside resources to assist us in identifying the solutions to the identified problems and their

causes. Most of the activities suggested in this chapter can best be described as an **external scanning process**. Our goal here, then, is to shift the conversation from framing the problem to finding a solution. That is to say, the aim of this chapter is to help you answer the question: *Given the problem we have framed, what in the **world** can we do to solve it?*

Sorting through the world of possible solutions to a problem in a school is a daunting task to say the least. Some of the tools that have been used throughout this manuscript can, once again, help to rationally limit the task somewhat. For example, the Four Common Places of Education can not only help us find root causes, but also give us a framework for finding a solution. Our task is to reflect critically on each possible solution and use data to eliminate some and focus in on the others. The possible explanations, combinations, and permutations are many. Nonetheless, the only way to successfully solve the problem is to painstakingly work through the array of possibilities. Fortunately, school improvement teams committed to creating an effective learning-centered system can find hope in the fact that many solutions are fairly simple—it's the implementation that's problematic. But we will discuss that issue in the next chapter.

In addition to the Four Common Places, the Correlates of Effective Schools have been presented as an interdependent set of variables that, taken together, represent the organizational leading indicators of learning. In the previous chapter, we presented ways to assess the stakeholders' perceptions of the presence or absence, strength or weakness of each of the Correlates. The Correlates of Effective Schools have also been used by many researchers and writers as a way of classifying and categorizing school and classroom strategies for improving student achievement. Therefore, the Correlates can serve as a bridge that can be used to move from framing the problem to seeking possible solutions.

Scanning for Effective Solutions

When looking for effective solutions, the members of the school improvement team should be guided by several questions.

- Is the proposed solution truly responsive to the problem?

- Is there supportive evidence that speaks to the effectiveness of the solution in other settings?

- Is the proposed solution feasible? That is, could the school effectively implement that solution if adopted?

- Is the proposed solution desirable? What might be the "side effects" (intended and unintended) of the solution?

- Can staff support the implementation steps?

- Finally, can the solution be generalized across the whole school and sustained over time?

These criteria and any others should be agreed upon *before* specific solutions are analyzed and discussed. Only then will the leadership team and the various stakeholder groups be able to examine possible solutions from a common understanding.

Four different scanning strategies for generating solutions are offered below. No one strategy is intrinsically better than any other; some strategies will work better in certain situations, while some will be more effective in other situations. Generally speaking, more than one strategy should be used to better ensure that the best possible decisions are made.

Strategy #1: Ask the Stakeholders.

Different stakeholder groups (teachers, support staff, parents) can offer different perspectives on the school and its problems. Here again, no stakeholder group can claim to have the only correct perspective on the problems. For example, teachers may claim that the solution to improved reading achievement is increased parent support. Parents may claim that the key to improved reading is better teacher communication with parents. In all probability, both stakeholder groups are correct to some degree and thus add valuable input to the discussion.

Many of the data gathering tools described earlier in this book could be adapted to help solicit suggestions and recommendations from one or more of the stakeholder groups. For example, teachers could be asked to use brainstorming to get everyone's perspective and then assess whether there is some consensus among the group members. Parents could be surveyed regarding what they believe could be done to solve the problems and which solutions they most strongly support.

The key point here is that solutions to the school's problems could come from anywhere and anyone. A school team should not take the view that valid solutions can't start in or around the school itself. On the other hand, the school team cannot let itself get trapped into believing that the best possible solutions can only be internally generated.

Strategy #2: Examine the Research.

In the past, research and "proven practices" played a minor or even nonexistent role in the choosing of new educational strategies and programs. Today, however, many states and the Federal Title I program require school improvement plans to be guided by research. The problem that school leadership teams now face is how to access the research that is most useful and informative given the limitations they face.

Most school improvement leadership teams have to perform this function in addition to all their regular duties. As a result, time is always an issue. It is both naive and unrealistic to expect members of the school leadership team to leave the school, travel to the nearest college or university library, and spend endless hours reading research journals. Fortunately, Internet technology makes it possible for school leadership teams to access both foundational and the most recent research information from anywhere, school or home. One example is the Effective Schools League, a membership service that contains an ever-growing database of well over 1,000 research summaries that can be searched by title, author, topic, keyword, or Effective Schools Correlate. Each summary addresses three questions: *What did the researcher do? What did the researcher find? What are possible implications for school improvement?* While reading a brief summary of a major research study can never replace a more careful reading of the complete document, the summaries do provide a manageable alternative. In addition, the Effective Schools League provides ongoing, threaded discussions around critical topics. Every member of the League has access to these rich conversations and every member is encouraged to contribute to them.

The Effective Schools League is an example—one I'm proud of—where the Internet makes it possible for the leaders of school improvement to have research information in a timely fashion. There are many other Internet sites that post research and proven practices. Some of these sites are free to anyone, while others—like the League—require a fee for service. Clearly, the Internet can reduce the bottleneck of finding and reading the relevant research. Who knows where the technology may allow us to go in connecting the knowledge-generating community with those that need that knowledge in the future!

Strategy #3: Benchmark Against Successful Schools.

Earlier in this book we discussed benchmarking as a tool to measure your school's progress in relation to past performance. Another way to use benchmarking is to find those organizations that are doing work similar to ours, but who seem to have discovered a more effective way of doing the work. Other organizations have found it beneficial to compare these proven practices with current practices and use the resulting discrepancy to suggest ways to improve. The notion is that most organizations could improve their own productivity if they simply tried to "level up" to those who do the task the best.

The Effective Schools history is replete with case studies of schools and school districts that have improved their achievement significantly and sustained the improvements for a long period of time. *Closing the Achievement Gap, No Excuses*, a book written by Patricia Davenport and Gerald Anderson, describes the successful processes and results in Brazosport, Texas. This book and many others do a good job of "setting the standard"—allowing other schools seeking improvement to compare their strategies and programs to those of some of the best in the business.

School leadership teams should take it upon themselves or empower others to explore the world of proven practices and develop a profile of how the best are organized and how their practices differ from those seeking to improve. The history of Effective Schools Research is very much a history of school practices that have been found over and over to coincide with higher student achievement. The Correlates of Effective Schools represent one way to describe how schools that are closer to achieving the "learning for all" mission differ from the rest.

One Web site and group deserves special mention when it comes to both finding the more effective schools and documenting their practices: the Education Trust (edtrust.org). The EdTrust group has published several studies; the most notable is *Dispelling the Myth—High Poverty Schools with High Achievement*. Examining this study and others like it is an excellent place for a school leadership team to begin a productive benchmarking process. A great deal of time can be saved and many false starts avoided by examining the literature on proven practices and benchmarking their school against these practices.

The literature is not the only place to find proven practices. Perhaps a school in your district or in a nearby district has been extremely successful in achieving the "learning for all" mission. It would be very worthwhile to send a small "search party" to review that school's policies, practices, and procedures to find those that are appropriate to your school or that could be adapted to suit your needs.

Benchmarking should not be viewed as a "copy-cat" strategy for improving schools. The process does not suggest that practices that work one place can be imported to another in a mindless way and be expected to work as well. On the other hand, ignoring what does work in some or, in the case of Effective Schools, many places and over time would show poor judgment on the part of the leadership team.

Strategy #4: Use Invention and Pilot Projects.

So far we have suggested that the processes of reflection could seek the input of stakeholders (internal scanning), or examine the relevant research and benchmark against the proven practices of successful schools (external scanning). All of these strategies will be useful in our model of the continuous school improvement process. However, school leadership teams should not overlook the need to actually invent a solution that draws upon the information gathered from the other three strategies and test its effectiveness through a pilot project.

Advocates of the continuous improvement process often criticize education for not conducting pilot projects to assess and refine a change process in a limited and scaled-down setting. However, both invention and pilot projects are valuable strategies for helping schools to get better at getting better. For example, suppose the school is trying to improve student achievement in reading and they have put together several ideas grounded in research and best practice. The leadership team should be encouraged to pilot test the ideas and processes with a few students. If the pilot project approach is carefully deployed, the school will learn several valuable lessons. First, they will see if the approach adds value to the goal of improved reading achievement. Second, the team will likely find both intended and unintended consequences, some positive and some negative. The data from the pilot project will allow the team to do some revisions before moving to a broader implementation.

Some would argue that a small pilot group of six or seven students is too small to yield reliable evidence. At one level, this criticism is valid and should be used as a caution. School teams should not overstate or overgeneralize what was learned in the pilot setting. On the other hand, if a careful trial of the program does not yield improvement for the small group, why would we think it would be more effective for a larger group? Ordinarily, a carefully conducted pilot project represents a best case scenario since more of the variables can be controlled. If a strategy doesn't work under best case conditions, it is unlikely to be effective under normal field conditions.

Selecting Improvement Goals

The reflection processes described in this chapter are designed to culminate in selecting specific school improvement goals. Here are a few guidelines that will help the school leadership team to avoid some common mistakes.

> Fewer goals usually have a better chance of succeeding than many goals.

Experience suggests that it is difficult and confusing for a school to be actively pursuing more than about three goals at any one time. Therefore, the many possible goals that surface as a result of the various strategies described above must be prioritized and only the top three developed for full implementation at this time.

> If goals of equal value based on research and proven practices are being considered, perhaps the one that solicits the greatest excitement and support from the staff should be given first priority.

Human factors such as ownership and commitment should not be ignored when it comes to choosing among several good options. Remember, successful and sustained school improvement requires that the staff embrace the changes and implement them with quality and caring. Too often, top-down strategies for

school reform fail because the level of commitment and support from those responsible for implementation was lacking. Therefore, issues revolving around staff commitment and support should be considered when goals of equal validity and value are being considered. That said, however, there is one important caveat. As important as these human factors are, successful school improvement is not likely to result if the staff choose improvement goals with which they are completely comfortable. School improvement requires change and change requires us to stretch beyond our comfort zones. The school leadership team should take whatever steps they can to help staff feel as comfortable as possible, but uneasiness among the adults cannot be an acceptable excuse for failing to do the right thing for the students.

> Continuous improvement theory suggests that 80 percent of the improvement will result from 20 percent of the changes that are implemented.

School leadership teams should be reassured that if they select a few goals based on good information and develop high quality action plans, improvement will be substantial. Said another way, doing a few things and doing them well will likely yield the best results.

Writing Improvement Objectives

Improvement objectives should reflect all the work that has occurred to date. That is, effective improvement objectives will:

- Link back to the stated purpose or mission that expresses the core values of the school;

- Derive from a careful analysis of the current student outcome data which determine strengths and weaknesses;

- Be stated in terms of student learnings; and

- Be expressed not as a test score, but as a core body of knowledge to be learned. In other words, a test score is the *evidence* that an improvement objective is or is not being met. For example, an appropriate improvement goal for 4th grade math will be "students will master the essentials of the fourth-grade math curriculum," **not** "students will perform above the 40th percentile on the SAT."

These criteria should be tempered by a caution from Ron Edmonds (1982) that "no local school plan should depend on changes over which the local school does not have control."

Let's assume the leadership team has already framed the problem and supported it with data. The problem statement will look something like this:

> **Problem Statement**
>
> Over the past three years, girls have not mastered the essential mathematics learnings. Evidence indicates that an average of 40 percent of the girls in Grades 2 to 5 received less than a C grade in mathematics; in addition, an average of only 28 percent of fourth-graders achieved proficiency status on the mathematics portion of the state standardized test over the past 3 years.

The next step in the planning process is for the school improvement team to take each problem statement and write it as an improvement objective. Remember, improvement objectives should be written in terms of measurable student outcomes, and should be linked to the essential student learnings that come from the school's mission.

Some of the objectives will be long-term in nature and some will have short timelines. It is suggested that long-term objectives be expressed in terms of three-to-five years and shorter objectives, from several months to a year or less. Some objectives may be new for a school to undertake and others may be of a "maintenance" nature. The improvement objective should be a specific, measurable statement of what is to be accomplished by a given point in time.

A well-written improvement objective will communicate the same intended outcome to everyone who reads it. It should include four components which will answer the questions, WHO? DOES WHAT? WHEN? HOW WILL IT BE MEASURED?

- The WHO relates to the person or persons.

- DOES WHAT is that which is to be known or done.

- WHEN relates to a specific point in time when something will have been learned or done.

- HOW WILL IT BE MEASURED relates to assessment techniques.

Problem Statement written as an Improvement Objective

By the last week of June (insert year), at least 80 percent of the girls in Grades 2 to 5 will have mastered the essential mathematics learnings for their grade level. The evidence used will be end-of-year grades of C or higher in Grades 2 to 5, as well as a score of proficient on the mathematics portion of the state standardized test for fourth graders.

Q: WHO will perform?
A: 80 percent of the Grade 2 to 5 girls.

Q: WHAT activity will be performed?
A: Mastery of the essential mathematics learnings.

Q: WHEN will it be performed?
A: By the last week of June, (year).

Q: HOW will it be measured?
A: A letter grade of C or higher in mathematics for girls in grades 2 to 5 and a score of "proficient" on the fourth-grade math portion of the state standardized test.

Figure 15.1

KEY CONCEPTS

- Reflection includes an internal scanning process and an external scanning process.

- Through the external scanning process, the leadership team looks to the research and stakeholders for potential solutions to identified problems.

- The team should choose improvement goals carefully, since 80 percent of the improvement will come from 20 percent of the improvement efforts.

- Pilot projects are a credible way of testing our proposed solutions before full implementation.

- Improvement objectives specify **who** will do **what** by **when**, and **how it will be measured.**

Chapter 16

Plan

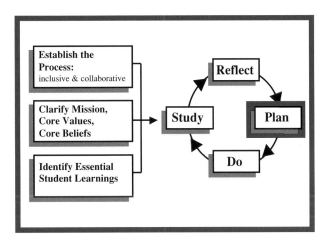

It has been said that those who fail to plan, plan to fail! This is certainly true when it comes to continuous school improvement. As a matter of fact, it is probably safe to say that *the vast majority of school improvement goals have never been implemented*. How can this be? While the improvement goals are written with the best of intentions, the implementation process is often either inadequate from the start, or is ignored or dropped. Why does school improvement planning have such a questionable track record when it comes to creating sustainable change in schools? There are several reasons.

Lack of a Clear Understanding of What the Intended Change Looks Like

School improvement often fails because the school improvement plan does not provide enough detail as to what is actually supposed to change in the school or classroom. For example,

school improvement plans might say that teachers should raise their expectations regarding learning for all students. But just because the leadership team knows what behaviors they are seeking, the rest of the staff does not. As a result, all staff may truly support the school leadership team's efforts and ultimate goals, but still not really know what they are supposed to do differently.

One of the tools that the leadership team should use to address this problem is to develop, distribute, and discuss a **"Now/Then" Matrix**. The first column of the matrix should detail current daily routines as they now operate in the school or classrooms. The description is intended to highlight what is supposed to change as we implement the improvement goal. In the second column, the leadership team should describe how the classroom or school is expected to operate once the intended changes have been successfully and fully implemented.

This approach can go a long way to clarify what is supposed to change and what the post-change classroom or school should be like. As a matter of fact, a good test of the school leadership team's readiness to move to the implementation phase of school improvement could be their ability to describe with some specificity what changes are being promoted.

Lack of a Detailed Implementation Plan

Most people have had experience with each of the following kinds of trips. One kind of trip starts with a clear destination, a timeline, and a detailed set of sequential milestones. The logic of this approach to travel is clear: if we meet the milestones in accordance with the timeline, we'll reach our destination in a timely manner. The second kind of trip is one where everyone jumps in the car and begins to drive without a clear destination in mind. There may be times when such free-spirited travel is enjoyable but, most of the time, such trips are very frustrating for those involved.

Although school improvement is an endless journey, it is not one that meanders willy-nilly wherever the political winds blow. By now you should have discerned that school improvement

---

"Now/Then" Matrix

Improvement Goal: By June of (   ), 80% of fourth-grade boys will master the essential learnings in the area of reading, as evidenced by attaining "proficient" status on the reading portion of the state standardized test.

Correlate: Time on Task   **Content Area:** Reading

Activity	Now	Then
Independent Reading	Independent reading occurs once or twice a week in grades 3-5.	All students will read independently for 20 minutes daily.
Small Group Work	Students currently do not have opportunities to discuss what they read with other students.	Students will form "literacy circles" of 4 or 5 students. The group will choose and read a book appropriate to reading level and meet weekly to discuss. Students will be provided a list of "starter questions" to guide their discussions.

Figure 16.1

planning and implementation is a very intentional process, with clear destinations along the way. Getting from the starting point to each destination requires a carefully thought-out set of sequenced action steps. Likewise, each step has an observable, measurable outcome that is to be achieved.

The school leadership team's ability to identify the milestones and place them in sequence and on an attainable timeline is vital if we are to reach our goals. A detailed map gives all those on the trip a clear picture of where they are and where they are going. When all those who are affected by the changes have a clear understanding of what is going to be happening and when, this goes a long way toward reducing their change anxiety.

Lack of a Monitoring Component in the Implementation Plan

Returning to the travel metaphor, it's one thing to say that we want to be at a certain place by a certain date, it's another to determine whether that milestone was met. For example, we may specify in our school improvement plan that, by the end of October, all teachers will know the research on teacher expectations and student achievement; however, without a monitoring system built in, we will never know if that objective or milestone was actually achieved.

Clearly, if subsequent steps in the process assume that the milestone was achieved, it is critical to the long-term success of the overall effort to be sure that each objective was achieved. To that

end, when the leadership team specifies the milestones, they should develop and describe what evidence will be used to monitor and evaluate the achievement of that milestone. Outlining the criteria for monitoring progress and judging success will give everyone involved a better understanding of the change and what it means for them.

Key Terms and Components of the Plan

Past experience with school teams and school improvement training has shown that different planning models define their terms somewhat differently. In an effort to avoid confusion, the key terms and components are presented below.

- **Educational Aims:** In this context, the broad educational purposes for which the school exists (reading, writing, arithmetic, and social responsibility for example) are going to be referred to as the school's educational aims.

- **Improvement Goals:** As defined in previous chapters, improvement goals will be those goals that are selected by the school leadership team as a result of their study of the problem. (Example: increasing the number of students performing at or above grade level in reading by 10%). In a previous section it was recommended that a school improvement plan focus on a few—no more than three—such improvement goals. Do not be deceived into thinking that three improvement goals will be easily managed.

- **Action Plans:** An action plan is defined as a description of the specific strategies to achieve the improvement goal with which it is linked. In this context, a single improvement goal could have *several* action plans associated with it. Given this fact, it is easy to see how even three improvement goals would likely produce a complex change effort in the school.

- **Action Plan Objective:** Each action plan will have a single objective associated with it. For example, given our reading improvement goal cited earlier, an action plan objective might be to establish a daily, schoolwide 20 minute silent reading period in the school.

- **Activities Matrix:** The activity matrix contains at least three essential pieces of information: a description of the tasks to be completed; the person or group responsible for completing the task; and a timeline that describes when the task is to be completed. Tasks should be listed in sequential order so everyone understands in what order the tasks are to be completed.

- **Monitoring Matrix:** The completion of the activity matrix produces a grid of the tasks to be completed; the monitoring matrix describes what information will be used to determine whether the activity was successfully completed. The monitoring matrix provides ongoing feedback to the leadership team so they can make adjustments when they are needed. For example, suppose that a note to inform parents about the new silent reading program did not get mailed on time; the team can then make a minor change in the timeline for the remaining events and activities.

- **Evaluating Improvement Goals—Evidence of Success:** Key to the implementation plan is a description of what data will be collected to determine whether the improvement goal had been achieved.

- **Other Helpful Information:** Since there is a variety of different planning formats, it's hard to say that one is better than all the others. School leadership teams should use whatever format they have been mandated to use by their district, state, or program (e.g., Title I). The approach to continuous school improvement recommended here can be adapted to accommodate virtually any planning template. Some templates require additional information, such as required resources or a budget. In addition, you may be required to provide a summary of the research used to inform the plan, or an educational impact statement that describes how the intended changes will likely affect other aspects of the school. Finally, you may be asked what other programs or services will need to be abandoned to accommodate the intended changes.

Activity and Monitoring Matrix Example

Improvement Goal: By June of (   ), the dropout rate for XYZ High School will be reduced to 4% by reducing the dropout rate by 3% each year over the next four years.

Correlate: Opportunity to Learn

Evidence of Need: Analysis of graduation records show that the average dropout rate over the past three years has been 12%. The dropout rate for the most current academic year was 12%. This compares with a statewide dropout rate of 4%.

Evidence of Success: Over the next four years, graduation rates of the current academic year will be compared with the previous academic year to assess if the one-year goal reduction of 3% has been met as well as progress-to-date on the overall Improvement Goal.

Action Plan Objective: Develop a comprehensive intervention system for students at-risk of dropping out.

Action Plan: YEAR 1

Activity Matrix			Monitoring Matrix	
Strategy	**Person Responsible**	**Timeline**	**Completion Evidence**	**Current Status— Adjustments Needed**
Develop criteria for identifying at-risk students	At-Risk Committee, chaired by Mr. Smith, counselor	Aug.—Oct.	Written report of criteria supported by research and data.	
Develop plan for faculty home visit program	At-Risk Committee	Oct.—Nov.	Written plan that includes who will be visited, techniques and methods for visits, who will visit training needs, and visitation follow-up plan.	
Train faculty for home visits	At-Risk Committee	Dec.	Report on training session: who attended, topics covered, attendee evaluation sheets.	
Conduct home visits	Mr. Smith coordinates	Jan.—June	Home visit report forms. Reports should include data of visit, who was met with, name of staff who conducted visit, other pertinent information concerning student issues and problems that may affect school attendance, engagement, and potential for dropping out.	

Figure 16.2

Mental Models of School Improvement Planning

Generally speaking, leadership teams develop action plans based on their mental models that represent their vision of school improvement. Three mental models typically guide the development of improvement action plans.

- School improvement can be thought of as a process designed to **change people**. Said another way, if our school is going to improve, the people who work here are going to have to change "the way they do things here." If that is your vision of school improvement, you may conclude that school improvement is more or less synonymous with staff development. With that mental model, the school leadership team would tend to focus their action plans on staff development strategies and events.

- A second mental model of school improvement is that school reform requires systemic change. If systemic change is the school leadership team's operating mental model of school reform, they would likely develop action plans targeted to the systems of the school. For example, report cards represent a grading and reporting **system.** Changing the current reporting system to one based on performance-based rubrics represents a substantial change in the system.

- A third possible mental model of school improvement is that school improvement represents planned or deliberate change. The world of change can be divided into that which is planned and that which is unplanned, often as a response to a crisis. It is much easier to unite people and build commitment to a change effort when responding to a crisis. It is far more difficult to unite people and build commitment and consensus when leaders are calling for change in the *absence* of an apparent crisis. As the CEO of Miliken Industries said after his company won the prestigious Baldridge Award, "good is often the enemy of better or best." Most schools are doing a pretty good job for many students. Staff may wonder "if we are already good, why work harder to get better?" But there is room for improvement in every school, and the challenge for the leadership team is to inspire the desire to be the best possible school that they can be. As a result of this third mental model, the leadership team will focus on consensus building and adult comfort levels, and proceed at a slower pace.

What is the lesson to be learned from these three different mental models that underpin school improvement efforts? The lesson is this: **the most effective school improvement in fact consists of all three.** Clearly, school improvement as presented here represents planned change, requiring both systemic and people change to be successful and sustainable. Therefore, school leadership teams must formulate action plans and activity matrices that are sensitive to the issues raised by each of the three different mental models of school improvement.

Critical Issues of Sustainable School Improvement

One of the core beliefs of this school improvement framework is that the school staff is already doing the best they know to do given the conditions in which they find themselves. If this belief is true and shared by the school leadership team, then staff will require new knowledge. Thus, the successful attainment of school improvement goals will require the school leadership team to address three critical issues in their improvement action plans.

- **Training and Technical Assistance:**

  Most school change that is likely to result in real and sustainable improvement in student achievement is going to require the staff to learn something they don't already know. Therefore, effective staff development will be key to effective school improvement. What makes staff development effective? First, it should be clearly tied to student achievement and the improvement goals we are trying to attain. Staff will be much more attuned to staff development that directly relates to what they are trying to do in the classroom rather than training that is nonspecific or vaguely goal-oriented. Second, a single in-service day is rarely enough time to learn and internalize new

knowledge to the point where it is easily implemented. Action plans for staff development must include a follow-up component that does two things—evaluate whether the new knowledge is being implemented as planned and to provide technical assistance to those who are struggling with that implementation.

- **Models of Success:**

  In addition to training and technical assistance, most school improvement efforts are likely to be more successful if the school staff and other affected stakeholders have access to "models of success." Written materials, video presentations, speakers, or school visitations allow the staff to see what the proposed changes look like in other settings. This helps to move the change forward.

  Furthermore, learning about, seeing, or visiting another place that is doing things in a way similar to what is being proposed seems to "demystify" the change process. When people see that "mere mortals" like us can do what is being called for, they generally feel more hopeful and positive toward change.

- **Networks of Support:**

  The school leadership team needs to be reminded that the action plans associated with any improvement objective should include the development of a time and place where staff can come together to talk. People involved in change need a safe forum where they can talk candidly about the "good," the "bad," and the "ugly" aspects of the change effort. Why are such networks helpful?

Schools as workplaces, especially for teachers, tend to be very isolated places. We know that teachers tend to spend less time talking to other teachers about teaching than doctors spend talking to other doctors about medicine, lawyers spend talking with other lawyers about law, etc. Because of this professional isolation, when a teacher encounters a problem or issue with the change process, their first response is often to retreat further into isolation, thinking that there is something wrong with *them*.

If the school team has created a safe place for candid conversation and built an atmosphere of trust where teachers can talk about problems, several outcomes can be anticipated—all of them good. First, talking about a problem with people you trust is, in and of itself, helpful. Second, the troubled teacher is probably not the only one having difficulty and that discovery is often reassuring. Third, it is very likely that the conversation will lead to some solutions to the problem (after all—as you may recall—*none of us is as smart as all of us!*).

Finally, it may turn out that such candid conversations may surface unintended negative consequences brought on by the change that were not anticipated by the school leadership team.

The critical issues of school improvement planning just discussed highlight the importance of several organizational factors. They include trust, teamwork, empowerment, and support of risk taking, to mention a few. Like the human experience itself, change is much more likely to succeed if the organism or organization is healthy at the outset of the change process. Deal and Kennedy have developed a set of scales that have proven useful in gauging the school readiness to support change. Marvin Fairman and his associates have developed and support a process called the Organizational Health Inventory. These tools and others like them can and should be used from time to time to "check up" on the health and well being of the school as a complex organization.

Soliciting Faculty and Community Endorsement

If, as has been suggested throughout this book, the staff and community have been continually involved in the school improvement planning process, then the presentation of the draft of the completed plan will contain no surprises. It is recommended, however, because of the importance of the activity, that special meetings be called to present the draft of the plan to staff, parents, community and students.

Leadership Challenge: Reflecting on School Climate for Planned Change

Part 1: Have each member of the leadership team rate the school on the following qualities and give an example that illustrates the rating.

		Weak		Moderate		Strong	
1.	Trusting	1	2	3	4	5	6

Example that illustrates rating: _____

2.	Trustworthiness	1	2	3	4	5	6

Example that illustrates rating: _____

3.	Teamwork	1	2	3	4	5	6

Example that illustrates rating: _____

4.	Supportive of Risk-taking	1	2	3	4	5	6

Example that illustrates rating: _____

5.	Sense of Sovereignty	1	2	3	4	5	6

Example that illustrates rating: _____

6.	Sense of Stewardship	1	2	3	4	5	6

Example that illustrates rating: _____

7.	Organizational Civility	1	2	3	4	5	6

Example that illustrates rating: _____

8.	Empowering	1	2	3	4	5	6

Example that illustrates rating: _____

Part 2: For those qualities rated weak, discuss as a team what might be done to strengthen that quality. Use one of the collaborative data-gathering tools from Chapter 8 and develop an action plan.

Figure 16.3

Ownership and Commitment

Mathews (1989) warns that it can be tempting for the school improvement team to believe it has brought closure to the task.

> *After all, they have engaged in an arduous task that has resulted in a written plan. They are likely to feel 'done.' If improvement is to be a driving force at the school, and the plan a living, breathing document that engages and empowers all adults at that place in the pursuit of even greater outcomes for kids, then the team is far from through. The school improvement team must secure the commitment of the faculty, the community, and all other interested constituencies in the plan. They must determine how to communicate and sell the plan, and realistically consider the obstacles to success and prepare ways to overcome them. The school improvement team must do so as a united front, and as a flexible team, recognizing that the likelihood of success is dependent on the degree to which the plan has meaning and is adopted by the adults who will make it happen.*

This ownership is critical to the future implementation of the plan. Also, public endorsement is symbolic because it illustrates approval for a change in the culture of the school and signifies a transition from planning to plan implementation.

However, "in the event that the staff cannot reach consensus on the plan, the . . . improvement process must move forward while the team strives for the highest level of agreement possible. Change processes must not be blocked by persons who want progress without change." (Lezotte and Bancroft, 1985)

Abandonment Targets

One of the greatest impediments to school improvement, especially in those situations where it is being mandated from above, is that nothing the school or teacher was doing is abandoned to make room for the proposed changes. When the issue of what goes—to make room for what is added—is ignored, teachers feel very frustrated and often defeated before the innovation actually gets underway. To correct this problem, any discussion of a change ought to be accompanied by a thoughtful consideration of how it will impact classroom and school practices and what current policies, procedures, or practices might be appropriately abandoned. Such abandonment decisions should be made thoughtfully, and should involve all or several of the teachers who teach that subject or grade level. In the final analysis, the chances of successfully implementing a change strategy will be significantly enhanced if the plan includes abandonment language that meets the following standard: teachers can understand clearly what is being added and what is being abandoned, and they believe that enough is being taken away to assure adequate time to add the new practices. This standard may seem obvious, but many efforts at school improvement falter or even fail because teachers perceive that the intended change represents an "add-on"—more work.

Communication Process

One of the responsibilities of the school improvement team is to assist in the ongoing communication needed for school improvement to progress from an idea of a few people to a vision widely shared by members of the organization and others whom the organization is intended to benefit. It will be necessary to plan how and when information about school improvement will be disseminated and determine what audience should be involved.

"Audiences" are usually identified as external or internal. The "external" groups are those that are outside the school, such as the local media (newspapers, radio, television), service organizations, and other community groups. The "internal" audience consists of those within the school system, such as administrators, teachers, support staff, bus drivers, custodians, cafeteria workers, etc. (SWEDL, 1990)

The SWEDL Guidebook (Southwest Educational Development Laboratory) makes the following suggestions:

For external audiences:

- Present a brief program to local service organizations.

- Start a newsletter to taxpayers or add a column to the school/district newsletter.

- Develop a slide/tape show.

- Write information stories for the local media.

- Hold an open house at school for the community.

- Publicize the mission statement

- Have school improvement on each school board agenda.

- Invite community members to attend school improvement meetings.

Another very important part of the public relations program is the establishment of ongoing communication about school improvement with internal audiences. Determine specific activities and personnel to facilitate communication within the school.

For internal audiences:

- Produce an internal newsletter for all staff members which includes their ideas on improving instruction as they relate to the plan.

- Write informational stories for the student newspaper.

- Encourage staff to present information during regular and special staff meetings.

- Hold informal gatherings for staff.

- Ask teachers to explain the plan to students.

- Hold periodic updates for staff and students.

The use of technology in communicating the plan has been discussed earlier and represents another important avenue for communicating with both internal and external audiences.

At this point, you should be able to develop a data-driven, research-based continuous school improvement plan with clear improvement goals, specific action plans tied to appropriate timelines, and an ongoing monitoring component to ensure its implementation. You will also have presented your plan to the faculty, parents, community, and other stakeholders (who have actually been involved in its development all along) and secured consensus and commitment to its implementation. Now, all you have to do is **DO IT**!

KEY CONCEPTS

- Many school improvement efforts fall short at implementation because of incomplete or poor planning. When developing the plan, use the following checklist to make sure your plan includes:

  - ❑ A clear picture of what the intended change looks like – What are we shooting for?
  - ❑ Understandable, achievable milestones by which to gauge progress toward the goal.
  - ❑ A reasonable timeline for reaching milestones and the ultimate goal.
  - ❑ Clear objectives for each milestone.
  - ❑ A monitoring system so those implementing the plan will be accountable, and the leadership team is able to adjust the timeline as needed to accommodate unforeseen situations.
  - ❑ A provision for training and technical assistance for staff who may need new skills to implement the plan.
  - ❑ Access to and time for stakeholders to view and learn about other successful models.
  - ❑ Time for stakeholders, particularly staff, to build networks of support to facilitate candid discussion and reflection on the school improvement process and activities.

- Although the finished plan should come as a surprise to no one, the leadership team must make a sincere effort to secure a public endorsement of the plan from faculty and the community. This builds ownership and commitment and increases the chances that stakeholders will implement the plan.

- Clear communication is the key to building commitment, and the leadership team should use multiple approaches to ensure that all stakeholders receive the necessary information in an appropriate manner.

Chapter 17

Do

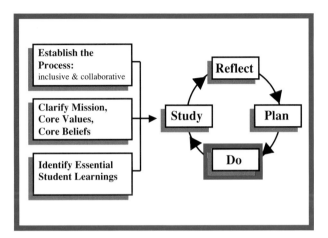

The previous chapter began with the statement, "those who fail to plan, plan to fail." This chapter could be subtitled, "plan the work, then work the plan." If the various tasks described throughout this manuscript have been completed, the school leadership team now has a well thought-out continuous school improvement plan. It's now time to **work the plan!**

We've noted that school improvement is simple, but not easy. Likewise, creating a school improvement plan by following the suggested guidelines may well turn out to have been easier than its actual implementation. There is no substitute for persistence and determination on the part of the school leadership team. However, experience in working with many schools as they struggled to implement their plans has yielded some "do's" and "don'ts." The following guidelines have proven to be helpful.

Improvement plans are not classified documents.

The school leadership team needs to recognize that their ultimate success as leaders depends on a committed group of followers willing to do what the leadership asks of them. The school board can give a group the authority to serve as the school improvement team but that, in and of itself, does not make them leaders. While authority is delegated from above, leadership is always delegated from below—from the followers.

Therefore, from the outset, it is critical for the leadership team to keep one eye on the level of commitment and support of those who will ultimately have to implement the plan. One of the best ways to sustain and nurture that commitment is by using an open, two-way communication system that assures that stakeholders are informed about the work of the leadership team *every step of the way*. School leadership teams that conduct their work in secret—even if it's good work—run the risk of engendering suspicion regarding what is going on. This suspicion can provide the fuel needed by the "nay-sayers" to undermine the change effort.

The degree to which the school leadership team must attend to the details of the two-way communication is, in no small way, dependent on the levels of trust and trustworthiness that characterize the organizational culture of the school. If the school has a history of distrust, then obviously more detailed and more frequent communications will be needed. On the other hand, if the school has a history of collaboration characterized by high levels of trust and trustworthiness, then less frequent communication will probably needed.

The school leadership team should set a goal that when the school plan is completed and ready for final discussion and approval, its contents will not be a surprise to any stakeholder. If the leadership team has effectively done its job, the stakeholders will have had prior knowledge and input into the process all along the way.

Involvement leads to commitment.

When the leadership team does a good job of providing ongoing opportunities for the stakeholders to be a part of the school improvement conversation, the stakeholders tend to be more committed to the process and the plan that it produces. Higher levels of involvement represent a "two-edged sword." On the one hand, it may seem more efficient to keep stakeholder involvement to a minimum. There is no doubt that one or two people working on their own can produce a plan in a short time. But if one or two people write the plan quickly but are unable to get the "buy-in" from the stakeholders who must implement it, what is the pay-off for this kind of efficiency?

On the other hand, when you share information with people, engage them in conversation around the information, and then ask them for feedback, it takes longer to get the plan done. In frustration, one principal asked, "How do you get everybody involved in the action and still have some action?" But in reality, the total amount of time it takes to develop a school plan that has the levels of commitment and support needed for its successful implementation doesn't change much. The leadership team can either rush the writing of the plan and spend more time building commitment after the fact, or the leadership team could design a process in which there is conversation all along the journey, thus reducing the need to "sell the plan" after the fact. Experience has shown that the latter method is more successful in building trust and commitment.

Expect the unexpected.

One reason that school improvement plans fail to be effectively implemented has to do with unexpected events and circumstances that arise in the school. We have recommended that a carefully crafted activity and monitoring matrix be developed that outlines milestones and timelines. Inevitably, the timelines become problematic because of unanticipated events that take precedence over the tasks in the improvement plan. Stephen Covey, in his best-selling book *Seven Habits of Highly Effective People* had a great way to describe this problem. Like people, organizations tend to focus on those things that they judge to be both urgent and important. For many people and schools, school improvement is seen as important, *but not urgent*. When this happens, the activities tend to be delayed or even postponed all together.

It is unrealistic to believe that schools could or would ignore the urgent and important issues of the day to keep focused on the school improvement plan. As a matter of fact, it would probably be both wrong and fatal to do so. However, it is not unrealistic to expect the school leadership team to do whatever it can to elevate school improvement on the priority list, to monitor the implementation steps and stages and, when necessary, make adjustments in either the work to be done or the timeline for doing it. If we are poised to expect the unexpected then such changes in the plan can be quickly and easily made.

Recognize the power of the System-In-Place.

As we mentioned in the chapter on Systems Theory, schools and school districts represent very complex and very stable systems. These systems are built upon certain core beliefs about the nature of the work to be done, students as learners, the role of education, and so on. Unfortunately, most educators have had little or no training in systems

thinking and how they quietly influence organizational and individual behavior. As a result, school leadership teams often grossly underestimate the power and momentum of the system-in-place to do again tomorrow what it did yesterday.

For example, for some schools that have been mandated to develop a school plan, the plan itself becomes the by-product of ritualistic behavior whose goal was simply to complete a satisfactory plan—meet the mandate—rather than truly improve the school. Since many of the mandating agencies lack the ability to monitor the implementation of plans, they focus on the plan as evidence of school improvement. The system-in-place, absent any real accountability, is then able to maintain the status quo and avoid any real substantive change.

Hopefully, providing some background in systems theory and calling specific attention to the power of the system-in-place will serve to alert the school leadership team to the task at hand. The momentum of the system-in-place is the enemy of change. Those leading the change effort should always overestimate rather than underestimate the power of that system to resist change and plan accordingly.

Attend to the feedback.

During the plan development process, the leadership team was asked to develop a monitoring matrix designed to "shadow" the various activities that made up the activities matrix. The intent of the monitoring matrix is to collect feedback information regarding whether a scheduled activity or event was successfully implemented.

Beyond monitoring planned activities to determine whether the plan is being successfully implemented as intended, the leadership team must be prepared to adjust the plan based on feedback from the stakeholder groups. For example, suppose that the activity matrix included a three-hour in-service for teachers on the new methods of classroom assessment. If the monitoring revealed that many teachers did not understand the new assessment model well enough to implement it, then an adjustment is needed.

Celebrate milestones big and small.

These things have become clear:

- School improvement is serious business.

- School improvement is not easy.

- Sustaining the improvement changes when they run against the status quo of the system-in-place is going to take a great deal of organizational energy.

As a result, it is to be expected that the leadership team, as well as other affected stakeholders, will grow weary as time goes on. How can the leadership team recharge its energy level and that of others involved in the implementation steps? One answer that is often overlooked is to *celebrate*.

Planned celebrations can serve several important functions. First, celebrations provide an enjoyable way to refocus the group. If the celebration highlights where the school has been, where it is now, and where it is going, it helps people to envision the "big picture."

Second, when supported with observable, measurable data that documents the progress being made, celebrations empower the group with new energy and inspire them to rededicate themselves to the goals. For example, most of us have had the experience of trying to lose weight at some time. Remember how energizing it felt to stand on the scale and see clear, objective evidence that we were making progress toward our goal. The same thing happens in the context of celebrating real progress in our school improvement efforts.

Third, celebrations can serve as a clear signal to those who are only marginally committed to the improvement process that the school is very serious about its commitment to successful implementation of the improvement plan. For those who had originally taken a "wait-and-see" attitude, the celebrations may help to deepen their commitment.

Four, celebrations are designed to be "fun." They need not be expensive, time consuming, or extravagant. They just need to be. An enjoyable celebration can also serve as a place where people can "let down" a bit and speak about the good and bad of the improvement process.

Schools have a long history of celebrating student accomplishments. Schools do less well when it comes to celebrating accomplishments of the adults in the school. I once heard a teacher react to being nominated by her principal as teacher of the year by asking, "What did I do to upset you?" For some reason, educators do not tend to celebrate their successful colleagues. Few schools make a point of celebrating goal attainment.

When we set out to change the school and the change impacts virtually everyone in the school to some extent, we need to celebrate progress toward those goals. In one school district, the superintendent would make a big deal out of bringing the state assessment results to any school that showed improvement. He would always come armed with cake and ice cream for the staff.

KEY CONCEPTS

- **Use the plan.** Consult it often. Keep it at the forefront of all discussion.

- **Share the story.** Keep everyone informed and involved throughout the planning process and make the final plan accessible to all interested stakeholders.

- Beware of the system-in-place.

- Be prepared to adjust the plan based on feedback from the implementers. Keep your eye on the goal, but be flexible in light of the unexpected.

- **Celebrate!** You've earned it.

Chapter 18

Putting It All Together

As you can see change is simple—it's just not easy! Remember, each school is ideally suited to producing the results it is currently getting. If stakeholders are satisfied with the current student achievement results, they will probably consider change unwarranted and unnecessary. It will be up to the leadership team to provide the data and the research to convince stakeholders that every school must continually strive to improve. The leadership team must present the information in such a way as to inspire first the desire to change, and then the sustained commitment to the change process. The guiding principles that have been suggested throughout this book should help you to meet the challenge of change and increase your chance for success.

A few improvement goals supported by well thought-out action plans properly sequenced and supported is a key to successful school improvement. But schools not only have to get better, *they have to get better at getting better*. Creating the organizational culture that supports continuous school improvement will be the key to the long-term sustainable success of public education. Unfortunately, schools have a long history of not investing in a system of continuous improvement. As a result, institutionalizing the philosophy of continuous improvement, like first learning to type or keyboard, is initially going to seem slow, painstaking, and arduous. Take heart, continuous improvement, like learning to type, will become easier and more natural once the processes become internalized by the educators who work in the school.

Final Thoughts

We end this book on continuous school improvement with a good news/bad news message. First the good news. At this point, the school leadership team has numerous reasons to be proud of its accomplishments. A great deal of time, talent, and effort has been expended all along the way. For all those reasons, the leadership team should feel proud when we come to the end of the implementation process. That's the good news!

Now for the bad news: continuous school improvement is, by definition, an endless journey. So even though we have completed one full cycle of school improvement planning and implementation, the journey is far from over. As a matter of fact, the evaluation data that is collected as part of the monitoring process represents the first step in the next "Study" phase of the continuous improvement cycle.

Now the leadership team can begin framing second generation problems with clear evidence of progress in hand and repeat the key aspects of the Study > Reflect > Plan > Do Cycle again.

At this point, the leadership team would be well advised to step back from the entire process and engage in a self-assessment process. The goal would be to determine whether the mission and core values should be amended given the changing context of education, and whether the focus of recent efforts is still appropriate. This is the point in the continuous improvement process that the leadership team asks itself those critical questions designed to help them get better at getting better.

Every time the school and the leadership repeats the Study > Reflect > Plan > Do Cycle, the process becomes more familiar to the staff and other stakeholders. After several trips through the continuous school improvement cycle, the process will become like second nature to the staff and other stakeholders. The school will evolve from an educational institution to a community of learners, where all are valued, and "learning for all" is the norm.

I would like to paraphrase Robert Hutchins from his book *The Conflict in Education in a Democratic Society*:

> *Perhaps the greatest idea that America has given the world is education for all. The world is entitled to know whether this idea means that everybody can be educated or simply that everyone must go to school.*

My dear colleagues, we have everyone going to school. The question is this: *can we truly educate a larger and larger percentage of the population, while taking the whole of the population to higher and higher standards?* I sincerely believe that we can. To do so will require change in the system-in-place. I believe and hope that the ideas put forth in this manuscript can, in some small way, serve to clear the path and make the journey a little less tenuous and success a little more likely.

Appendices

Correlates of Effective Schools: The First and Second Generation

A number of schools have been relying on effective schools research as the framework for their school improvement program. After three or four years, many claim that they have successfully met the criteria described in the research on the correlates of effective schools. These educators ask if there is anything that comes after, or goes beyond, these standards.

The concept of second generation correlates attempts to incorporate the recent research and school improvement findings and offers an even more challenging developmental stage to which schools committed to the **Learning for All** mission ought to aspire.

There are two underlying assumptions to keep in mind: First, school improvement is an endless journey. Second, the second generation correlates cannot be implemented successfully unless the first generation correlate standards are present in the school. In one sense, the second generation correlates represent a developmental step beyond the first and, when successfully accomplished, will move the school even closer to the mission of **Learning for All**.

1. **Safe and Orderly Environment**

   The First Generation: In the effective school there is an orderly, purposeful, businesslike atmosphere which is free from the threat of physical harm. The school climate is not oppressive and is conducive to teaching and learning.

   The Second Generation: In the first generation, the safe and orderly environment correlate was defined in terms of the absence of undesirable student behavior (e.g., students fighting). In the second generation, the concept of a school environment conducive to **Learning for All** must move beyond the elimination of undesirable behavior. The second generation will place increased emphasis on the presence of certain desirable behaviors (e.g., cooperative team learning). These second generation schools will be places where students actually help one another.

   Moving beyond simply the elimination of undesirable behavior will represent a significant challenge for many schools. For example, it is unlikely that a school's faculty could successfully teach its students to work together unless the adults in the school model collaborative behaviors in their own professional working relationships. Since schools as workplaces are characterized by their isolation, creating more collaborative/cooperative environments for both the adults and students will require substantial commitment and change in most schools.

First, teachers must learn the "technologies" of teamwork. Second, the school will have to create the "opportunity structures" for collaboration. Finally, the staff will have to nurture the belief that collaboration, which often requires more time initially, will assist the schools to be more effective and satisfying in the long run. But schools will not be able to get students to work together cooperatively unless they have been taught to respect human diversity and appreciate democratic values. These student learnings will require a major and sustained commitment to multicultural education. Students and the adults who teach them will need to come to terms with the fact that the United States is no longer a nation with minorities. We are now a nation of minorities. This new reality is currently being resisted by many of our community and parent advocacy groups, as well as by some educators.

2. Climate of High Expectations for Success

The First Generation: In the effective school there is a climate of expectation in which the staff believe and demonstrate that all students can attain mastery of the essential school skills, and the staff also believe that they have the capability to help all students achieve that mastery.

The Second Generation: In the second generation, the emphasis placed on high expectations for success will be broadened significantly. In the first generation, expectations were described in terms of attitudes and beliefs that suggested how the teacher should behave in the teaching-learning situation. Those descriptions sought to tell teachers how they should initially deliver the lesson. High expectations meant, for example, that the teacher should evenly distribute questions asked among all students and should provide each student with an equal opportunity to participate in the learning process. Unfortunately, this "equalization of opportunity," though beneficial, proved to be insufficient to assure mastery for many learners. Teachers found themselves in the difficult position of having had high expectations and having acted upon them—yet some students still did not learn.

In the second generation, the teachers will anticipate this and they will develop a broader array of responses. For example, teachers will implement additional strategies, such as reteaching and regrouping, to assure that all students do achieve mastery. Implementing this expanded concept of high expectations will require the school as an organization to reflect high expectations. Most of the useful strategies will require the cooperation of the school as a whole; teachers cannot implement most of these strategies working alone in isolated classrooms.

High expectations for success will be judged, not only by the initial staff beliefs and behaviors, but also by the organization's response when some students do not learn. For example, if the teacher plans a lesson, delivers that lesson, assesses learning and finds that some students did not learn, and still goes on to the next lesson, then that teacher didn't expect the students to learn in the first place. If the school condones through silence that teacher's behavior, it apparently does not expect the students to learn, or the teacher to teach these students.

Several changes are called for in order to implement this expanded concept of high expectations successfully. First, teachers will have to come to recognize that high expectations for student success must be "launched" from a platform of teachers having high expectations for self. Then the school organization will have to be restructured to assure that teachers have access to more "tools" to help them achieve successful **Learning for All**. Third, schools, as cultural organizations, must recognize that schools must be transformed from institutions designed for "instruction" to institutions designed to assure "learning."

3. Instructional Leadership

The First Generation: In the effective school the principal acts as an instructional leader and effectively and persistently communicates that mission to the staff, parents, and students. The principal understands and applies the characteristics of instructional effectiveness in the management of the instructional program.

The Second Generation: In the first generation, the standards for instructional leadership focused primarily on the principal and the administrative staff of the school. In the second generation, instructional leadership will remain important; however, the concept will be broadened and leadership will be viewed as a dispersed concept that includes all adults, especially the teachers. This is in keeping with the teacher empowerment concept; it recognizes that a principal cannot be the only leader in a complex organization like a school. With the democratization of organizations, especially schools, the leadership function becomes one of creating a "community of shared values." The mission will remain critical because it will serve to give the community of shared values a shared sense of "magnetic north," an identification of what this school community cares most about. The role of the principal will be changed to that of "a leader of leaders," rather than a leader of followers. Specifically, the principal will have to develop his/her skills as coach, partner and cheerleader. The broader concept of leadership recognizes that leadership is always delegated from the followership in any organization. It also recognizes what teachers have known for a long time and what good schools have capitalized on since the beginning of time: namely, expertise is generally distributed among many, not concentrated in a single person.

4. **Clear and Focused Mission**

The First Generation: In the effective school there is a clearly articulated school mission through which the staff shares an understanding of and commitment to the instructional goals, priorities, assessment procedures and accountability. Staff accept responsibility for students' learning of the school's essential curricular goals.

The Second Generation: In the first generation, the effective school mission emphasized teaching for **Learning for All**. The two issues that surfaced were: Did this really mean all students or just those with whom the schools had a history of reasonable success? When it became clear that this mission was inclusive of all students especially the children of the poor (minority and non-minority), the second issue surfaced. It centered itself around the question: Learn what? Partially because of the accountability movement and partially because of the belief that disadvantaged students could not learn higher-level curricula, the focus was on mastery of mostly low-level skills.

In the second generation, the focus will shift toward a more appropriate balance between higher-level learning and those more basic skills that are truly prerequisite to their mastery. Designing and delivering a curriculum that responds to the demands of accountability, and is responsive to the need for higher levels of learning, will require substantial staff development. Teachers will have to be better trained to develop curricula and lessons with the "end in mind." They will have to know and be comfortable with the concept of "backward mapping," and they will need to know "task analysis." These "tools of the trade" are essential for an efficient and effective "results-oriented" school that successfully serves all students.

Finally, a subtle but significant change in the concept of school mission deserves notice. Throughout the first generation, effective schools proponents advocated the mission of teaching for **Learning for All**. In the second generation the advocated mission will be **Learning for All**. The rationale for this change is that the "teaching for" portion of the old statement created ambiguity (although this was unintended) and kept too much of the focus on "teaching" rather than "learning." This allowed people to discount school learnings that were not the result of direct teaching. Finally, the new formulation of **Learning for All** opens the door to the continued learning of the educators as well as the students.

5. **Opportunity to Learn and Student Time on Task**

The First Generation: In the effective school teachers allocate a significant amount of classroom time to instruction in the essential skills. For a high percentage of this time students are engaged in whole class or large group, teacher-directed, planned learning activities.

The Second Generation: In the second generation, time will continue to be a difficult problem for the teacher. In all likelihood, the problems that arise from too much to teach and not enough time to teach it will intensify. In the past, when the teachers were oriented toward "covering curricular content" and more content was added, they knew their response should be to "speed-up." Now teachers are being asked to stress the mission that assures that the students master the content that is covered. How are they to respond? In the next generation, teachers will have to become more skilled at interdisciplinary curriculum and they will need to learn how to comfortably practice "organized abandonment." They will have to be able to ask the question, "What goes and what stays?" One of the reasons that many of the mandated approaches to school reform have failed is that, in every case, the local school was asked to do more! One of the characteristics of the most effective schools is their willingness to declare that some things are more important than others; they are willing to abandon some less important content so as to be able to have enough time dedicated to those areas that are valued the most.

The only alternative to abandonment would be to adjust the available time that students spend in school, so that those who need more time to reach mastery would be given it. The necessary time must be provided in a quality program that is not perceived as punitive by those in it, or as excessive, by those who will have to fund it. These conditions will be a real challenge indeed!

If the American dream and the democratic ideal of educating everyone is going to move forward, we must explore several important policies and practices from the past. Regarding the issue of time to learn, for example, if the children of the disadvantaged present a "larger educational task" to the teachers and if it can be demonstrated that this "larger task" will require more time, then our notions of limited compulsory schooling may need to be changed. The current system of compulsory schooling makes little allowance for the fact that some students need more time to achieve mastery. If we could get the system to be more mastery-based and more humane at the same time, our nation and its students would benefit immensely.

6. Frequent Monitoring of Student Progress

The First Generation: In the effective school student academic progress is measured frequently through a variety of assessment procedures. The results of these assessments are used to improve individual student performance and also to improve the instructional program.

The Second Generation: In the first generation, the correlate was interpreted to mean that the teachers should frequently monitor their students' learning and, where necessary, the teacher should adjust his/her behavior. Several major changes can be anticipated in the second generation. First, the use of technology will permit teachers to do a better job of monitoring their students' progress. Second, this same technology will allow students to monitor their own learning and, where necessary, adjust their own behavior. The use of computerized practice tests, the ability to get immediate results on homework, and the ability to see correct solutions developed on the screen are a few of the available "tools for assuring student learning."

A second major change that will become more apparent in the second generation is already under way. In the area of assessment the emphasis will continue to shift away from standardized norm-referenced paper-pencil tests and toward curricular-based, criterion-referenced measures of student mastery. In the second generation, the monitoring of student learning will emphasize "more authentic assessments" of curriculum mastery. This generally means that there will be less emphasis on the paper-pencil, multiple-choice tests, and more emphasis on assessments of products of student work, including performances and portfolios.

Teachers will pay much more attention to the alignment that must exist between the intended, taught, and tested curriculum. Two new questions are being stimulated by the reform movement and will dominate much of the professional educators' discourse in the second generation: "What's worth knowing?" and "How will we know when they know it?" In all likelihood, the answer to the first question will become clear relatively quickly, because we can reach agreement that we want our students to be self-disciplined, socially responsible, and just. The problem comes with the second question, "How will we know when they know it?" Educators and citizens are going to have to come to terms with that question. The bad news is that it demands our best thinking and will require patience if we are going to reach consensus. The good news is that once we begin to reach consensus, the schools will be able to deliver significant progress toward these agreed-upon outcomes.

7. Home-School Relations

The First Generation: In the effective school parents understand and support the school's basic mission and are given the opportunity to play an important role in helping the school to achieve this mission.

The Second Generation: During the first generation, the role of parents in the education of their children was always somewhat unclear. Schools often gave "lip service" to having parents more actively involved in the schooling of their children. Unfortunately, when pressed, many educators were willing to admit that they really did not know how to deal effectively with increased levels of parent involvement in the schools.

In the second generation, the relationship between parents and the school must be an authentic partnership between the school and home. In the past when teachers said they wanted more parent involvement, more often than not they were looking for unqualified support from parents. Many teachers believed that parents, if they truly valued education, knew how to get their children to behave in the ways that the school desired. It is now clear to both teachers and parents that the parent involvement issue is not that simple. Parents are often as perplexed as the teachers about the best way to inspire students to learn what the school teaches. The best hope for effectively confronting the problem—and not each other—is to build enough trust and enough communication to realize that both teachers and parents have the same goal—an effective school and home for all children!

Essential Student Learnings
Example #1

A. Academic Learning:

1. Reading — reading concepts and skills necessary for successful middle school performance and to permit reading for personal enjoyment.

2. Writing and Speaking — writing and speaking skills required for successful middle school performance.

3. Mathematics — mathematics concepts and skills necessary to take 8th grade pre-algebra.

4. Geography — geography skills and concepts necessary for global awareness.

5. Science — to be developed.

6. Fine Arts — to be developed.

7. Study Skills — to be developed.

8. Other

B. Social/Emotional Behaviors and Attitudes including:

1. Responsibility for learning.

2. Participation in co-curricular programs.

3. Courtesy, respect, and concern for others.

4. Demonstration of self-discipline.

5. Other

NOTE: Specific essential student learnings in each of these areas are either available or will be developed as part of our improvement process.

Essential Student Learnings
Example #2

Students will:

- comprehend what they read
- write and speak with clarity and correctness
- solve mathematical problems
- use scientific facts and principles
- understand past and present cultures
- develop habits which promote physical and emotional well-being
- demonstrate learning and problem solving skills
- show courtesy, respect, and concern for others
- assume a productive and responsible role in society

Essential Student Learnings
Example #3

A student:

1. Displays self-esteem as a learner and a person.

2. Exhibits cognitive learning:
    a. Masters essential skills.
    b. Learns on an extended basis.
    c. Progresses from low to high cognitive levels.

3. Possesses process skills:
    a. Solves problems.
    b. Communicates effectively.
    c. Makes decisions in a logical, mature manner.
    d. Demonstrates accountability.
    e. Understands group processes.

4. Learns in a self-directed manner.

5. Shows concern for others.

6. Demonstrates emotional, social, and physical well being.

Essential Student Learnings Example #4

General Academic Skills

- Demonstrate the ability to use effectively the communication skills of reading, writing, speaking, and listening.

- Demonstrate the ability to understand and apply basic mathematical functions and principles in real-life problem-solving situations.

- Demonstrate knowledge and understanding of the basic principles, concepts, and language of the natural sciences.

- Demonstrate a functional level of computer and technological literacy.

- Demonstrate knowledge and understanding of the history, geography, government, and economic systems of the United States and other countries.

Problem-Solving Skills

- Demonstrate skills in individual and group problem solving and decision making.

- Demonstrate the ability to identify and critically analyze problems.

Social Literacy and Responsibility

- Demonstrate an understanding of one's rights and responsibilities in a democratic society.

- Demonstrate an understanding of the implications of the cultural diversity of this country.

- Demonstrate knowledge and understanding of world cultures.

- Demonstrate the knowledge and understanding necessary for environmentally responsible behavior.

- Demonstrate an understanding of the arts as an expression of culture and personal creativity.

Personal Effectiveness

- Demonstrate the interpersonal skills necessary to be personally and professionally effective.

- Demonstrate the ability to develop and implement plans for achieving personal and career goals.

- Demonstrate knowledge of effective employment skills.

- Demonstrate knowledge and understanding of maintaining personal, emotional, and physical health.

- Demonstrate an understanding of the personal and economic responsibilities of adulthood.

- Demonstrate the skills necessary to be an effective life-long learner.

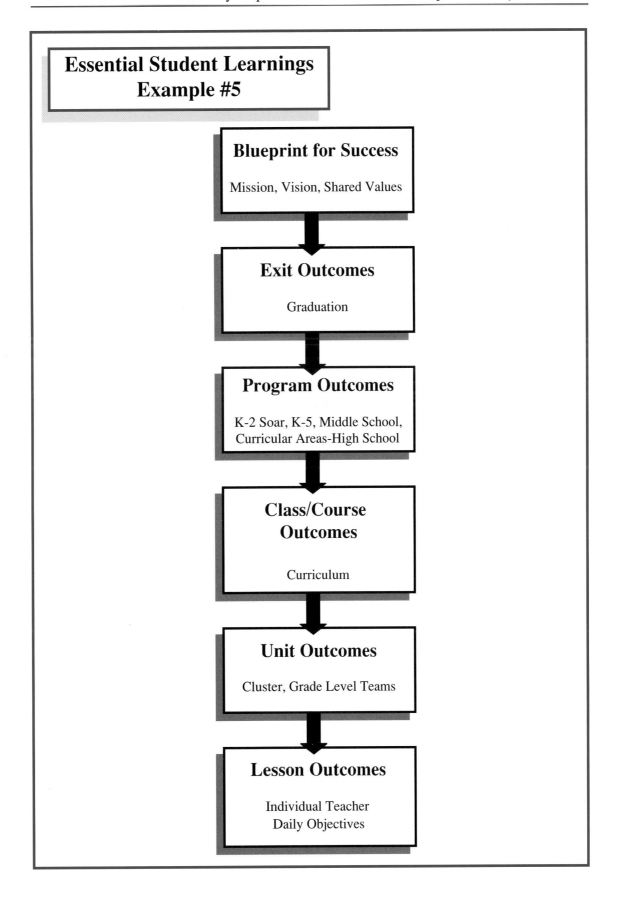

**Essential Student Learnings
Example #5**

Blueprint for Success

Mission, Vision, Shared Values

Exit Outcomes

Graduation

Program Outcomes

K-2 Soar, K-5, Middle School,
Curricular Areas-High School

**Class/Course
Outcomes**

Curriculum

Unit Outcomes

Cluster, Grade Level Teams

Lesson Outcomes

Individual Teacher
Daily Objectives

Online Tools from Effective Schools Products

Gotta do a Needs Assessment?
Use Reality Check: The Online Needs Assessment Tool

What are your school's strengths and weaknesses?
What concerns are facing your teachers?
How do parents and the community view your school?

It could take you days, weeks, or even months to come up with the right surveys to find the answers to these questions. But with Reality Check, an exciting online tool from Effective Schools Products, you can quickly and easily design, administer, and analyze a survey for staff, parents, or students. This easy-to-use tool allows you to:

- Take the guesswork out of developing a survey. Reality Check offers you Larry Lezotte's "Getting Started" guide, as well as his staff, parent, and student template surveys.

- Develop a customized survey. Choose questions from Reality Check's searchable database of over 2,000 items categorized by the Correlates of Effective Schools; use them as written, modify them to suit your needs, or create entirely new ones.

- Create a survey that your stakeholders can take online. You can link it directly to your school or district web page or set up a computerized "survey station" at events and activities (e.g., parent night).

- Create a paper and pencil survey. If you're not ready for online surveys, you can print and distribute your survey in paper form. Reality Check allows you to format and personalize your survey for a custom professional look.

- Create your survey in English or Spanish. Online respondents can choose to respond in either language with the click of a button.

- Get instant results. Have the aggregated results from online respondents available instantly in both table and chart form with no need to hand-enter data. You can also download the results easily and quickly into a spreadsheet program for further analysis, including disaggregation of the data.

Now developing and processing a survey will take less time than ever. And Reality Check is cost-effective, too. Hiring an outside consultant could cost 10 times the purchase price or more!

Visit our website at www.effectiveschools.com for additional information.

Online Tools from Effective Schools Products

"School Improvement and Teaching Strategies must be based on 'proven practices'—and that means research!"
— Larry Lezotte

Effective Schools League

With the League, the tools and just-in-time information you need for effective school improvement are just a mouse-click away:

- Access to the Research. You could spend hundreds of hours surfing the web or pouring through journals, trying to gather relevant data. Or, you can access over 1,100 research studies on effective school improvement at one site—with 72 new studies added annually. Search by topic (e.g., effective instruction), title, author, or keyword (e.g., professional development).

- Tools for Staff Training. The League is the essential resource for schools and districts just beginning the journey of continuous school improvement, as well as for those who need to bring new staff into the continuous improvement mindset. You and your staff will find information on the Effective Schools Framework, the Correlates of Effective Schools, the Correlates as Leading Indicators, and more—all in one place.

- Opportunities to Network and Dialog. The League enables you to share questions, views, concerns, and information with colleagues across the nation and Canada, and keeps you apprised of current happenings in education, upcoming national and regional conferences, and the latest Effective Schools resources.

Visit our website at www.effectiveschools.com for additional information.

Planning Process Chart

Goal _____   Evidence of Need _____

_____   _____

Student Outcome _____   Evidence of Success _____

_____   _____

Strategies	Person Responsible for Implementing Strategy	Person Responsible for Measuring Progress of the Strategy	Resources Needed	Dates of Activity		Assessment Date(s) *When is progress to be measured?*	Criteria for Outcome Attainment & How Measured *How will we know the objective was attained?*
				Start	End		
1.							
2.							
3.							

Progress Checklist

Please check the progress of your building in the School Improvement Planning Process.

Activity	Completed	Continuing	Yet to be Done
1. Orientation			
2. Team Training			
3. Mission Statement			
4. Glossary/data sources identified			
5. Essential Student Learnings Determined			
6. Student Outcome Data Collected			
7. Data Disaggregated			
8. Summary of Correlate Strengths/ Weaknesses			
9. Student Outcome Improvement Objectives Determined			
10. Strategies/Activities Determined for Each Objective			

Suggested Timeline for Implementing the Effective Schools Continuous Improvement Process

-0 to 3 months

Exploring various models of continuous school improvement. Work to be completed by an adhoc committee. Goal to make a recommendation with supporting rationale to the entire school faculty for their endorsement.

Time Zero

School faculty, after orientation and discussion, formally adopts the Effective Schools Continuous Improvement Process.

0 – 1 month

Select the members of the Continuous School Improvement Team (CSIT).

2 – 4 months

Provide the CSIT with initial in-depth training in the processes and also plan and implement a schoolwide, stakeholder training. The staff training may or may not include an external consultant and trainer.

4 – 8 months

CSIT coordinates a series of process steps aimed at clarifying the school's mission, core beliefs and core values. The deliverable product would be the school's mission statement, a list of core beliefs and core values, and maybe an attached glossary of terms. Final process in this phase is to secure the endorsement of the various stakeholder groups.

6 – 9 months: STUDY

CSIT begins gathering and analyzing current and recent data to determine where the school is relative to its mission. These data would include, but are not limited to, state and local student assessment results disaggregated across the identifiable subgroups in the school. Furthermore, the CSIT coordinates further data gathering to "drill down" to the root causes of the achievement problems in the school. This step, when completed, answers the question: *How are we doing relative to achieving our mission?"*

9 –12 months: REFLECT

The CSIT engages in external scanning activities of research and proven practices to determine how to address the achievement issues. In addition, the CSIT also seeks input from the faculty and other stakeholders relative to their ideas and theories regarding how to solve the problems the school has identified.

The reflection phase will yield the improvement goals as the current focus of school improvement efforts.

10 – 14 months: PLAN

Once the improvement goals have been formulated, the CSIT will develop one or more action plans that will be used as the guide for their implementation. A significant part of the action plan would be the strategies that will be used throughout the implementation phase to formatively evaluate how the implementation phase is progressing.

12 – 18 months: DO

Under the careful monitoring of the CSIT, the improvement action plans will be implemented. Throughout the implementation phase, a variety of different data will be collected and analyzed. The aim of the data collection is to be sure that the elements of the plan were actually completed, and to evaluate their impacts on teachers, students, parents, and others.

Once a complete cycle has occurred, the CSIT now returns to the Study Phase to determine the impact of the first cycle, what new problems or issues have surfaced. The **Study > Reflect > Plan > Do Cycle** is repeated over and over. Once the cycle has become an ongoing part of the schools operations, the timelines will be able to be compressed and the process will become less rigid and less linear.

References

References

Ackoff, Russell L., *Creating the Corporate Future: Plan or Be Planned For*. Wiley, New York, New York, 1981.

Allen, Lew, "From Plaques to Practice: How Schools Can Breathe Life into Their Guiding Beliefs," *Phi Delta Kappan* 83, 4 (December 2001): 289-293.

Bailey, William J., *School-site Management Applied*. Technomic Publishing Company, Lancaster, Massachusetts, 1991.

Bernhardt, Victoria L., *Data Analysis for Comprehensive Schoolwide Improvement*. Eye on Education, New York, New York, 1998.

Blanchard, Ken and Sheldon Bowles, *Gung ho!* 1st ed. Morrow Publishing, New York, New York, 1998.

Blanchard, Ken and Sheldon Bowles, *High Five! The Magic of Working Together*. Harper Collins, New York, New York, 2001.

Blanchard, Ken, Donald Carew, and Eunice Parisi-Carew, *The One-Minute Manager Builds High Performing Teams*. 1st ed. Blanchard Training and Development, Escondido, California, 1990.

Bosak, Steve, "All Together Now: A guide through the collaborative technology jungle," *Electronic School: The School Technology Authority*. A supplement to *American School Board Journal* 187, 1 (January 2000): 34-37.

Bradburn, Norman, Seymour Sudman, and Associates, *Improving Interview Method and Questionnaire Design*. Jossey-Bass Publishers, San Francisco, California, 1979.

Brassard, Michael, *The Memory Jogger Plus+*. GOAL/QPC, Methuen, Massachusetts, 1989.

Brown, John L. and Cerylle A. Moffett, *The Hero's Journey: How Educators Can Transform Schools and Improve Learning*. Association for Supervision and Curriculum Development, Alexandria, Virginia, 1999.

Byham, William C., *ZAPP! in Education: How Empowerment Can Improve the Quality of Instruction, and Student and Teacher Satisfaction.* Fawcett Columbine, New York, New York, 1992.

Center for the Study of Systemic Reform in Milwaukee Public School, 1025 W. Johnson Street, Madison, Wisconsin, 53706 (http://www.wcer.wisc.edu/mps).

Chang, Richard Y. and Douglas D. Dalziel, *Continuous Improvement Tools in Education: Volume 1.* APQC Education Series, Irvine, California, 1999.

Chang, Richard Y. and Douglas D. Dalziel, *Continuous Improvement Tools in Education: Volume 2.* APQC Education Series, Irvine, California, 1999.

Covey, Stephen R., *7 Habits of Highly Effective People.* Simon & Schuster, New York, New York, 1989.

Davenport, Patricia and Gerald Anderson, Ed. D., *Closing the Achievement Gap: No Excuses.* APQC, Houston, Texas, 2002.

Deal, Terrance E. and Allan A. Kennedy, "Culture and School Performance," *Educational Leadership* 40, 5 (February 1983): 140-141.

Dispelling the Myth: High Poverty Schools Exceeding Expectations. Report of the Education Trust in cooperation with the Council of Chief State School Officers and partially funded by the U.S. Department of Education, Washington, D.C., 1999.

District Plan for School Improvement. Hillsdale (Michigan) Community Schools, 1991.

Dolan, W. Patrick, *Restructuring Our Schools: A Primer on Systemic Change.* Systems and Organizations, Kansas City, Missouri, 1994.

Edmonds, Ronald R., "Programs of School Improvement: An Overview," *Educational Leadership* 40, 3 (December 1982): 8-11.

Education Trust, 1725 K Street NW, Suite 200, Washington, D.C., 20006 (http://www.edtrust.org).

Erb, Thomas O. and Nancy M. Doda, *Team Organization: Promise-Practices and Possibilities.* National Education Association, Washington, D.C., 1989.

"Expanding Charter School Movement," *The State of Charter Schools 2000: Fourth-Year Report.* U.S. Department of Education, Washington, D.C., 2000 (http://www.ed.gov).

Fairman, Marvin F., Organizational Health: Diagnostic and Development Corporation, 3201 Shore View Drive, Highland Village, Texas, 75077 (http://www.organizationalhealth.com).

Finding Time for School Improvement. Middle Cities Education Association, Okemos, Michigan, 1996.

Fitz-Gibbon, Carol Taylor, and Lynn Lyons Morris, *How to Analyze Data.* Sage Publications, Newbury Park, California, 1987.

Francis, Dave and Don Young, *Improving Work Groups: A Practical Manual for Team Building.* University Associates, Inc., San Diego, California, 1979.

Fullan, Michael G., *The New Meaning of Educational Change.* Teachers College Press, New York, New York, 1991.

Gray, Barbara, *Collaborating: Finding Common Ground for Multiparty Problems.* Jossey-Bass, Inc., San Francisco, California, 1989.

Guidebook for the Educational Change Facilitator. Southwest Educational Development Laboratory (SWEDL), Austin, Texas, 1990.

Guthrie, Hal, Gary Mathews, et al., "Campus Improvement Planning: A Systemic Team Approach," (in two parts) *Instructional Leader* 2, 3 (June 1989): 1-9, and 2, 4 (August 1989): 1-11.

Henderson, Anne T., Carl L. Marburger, and Theodora Ooms, *Beyond the Bake Sale: An Educator's Guide to Working with Parents.* National Committee for Citizens in Education, Columbia, Maryland, 1989.

Hutchins, Robert Maynard, *Conflict in Education in a Democratic Society.* Greenwood Publishers Group, Westport, Connecticut, 1972.

Johnson, Ruth S., *Setting Our Sights: Measuring Equity in School Change.* The Achievement Council, Chico, California, 1996.

Larson, Carl E. and Frank M.J. LaFasto, *TeamWork: What Must Go Right / What Can Go Wrong.* Sage Publications, Newbury Park, California, 1989.

Leedy, Paul D., *Practical Research Planning and Design.* 3rd ed., Macmillan Publishing Company, New York, New York, 1985.

Lezotte, Lawrence W., *Correlates of Effective Schools: The First and Second Generation.* Effective Schools Products, Okemos, Michigan, 1991.

Lezotte, Lawrence W., *Learning for All.* Effective Schools Products, Okemos, Michigan, 1997.

Lezotte, Lawrence W. and Barbara C. Jacoby, *A Guide to the School Improvement Process based on Effective Schools Research*. Effective Schools Products, Okemos, Michigan, 1990.

Lezotte, Lawrence W. and Barbara C. Jacoby, *Sustainable School Reform: The District Context for School Improvement*. Effective Schools Products, Okemos, Michigan, 1992.

Lezotte, Lawrence W. and Beverly A. Bancroft, "Growing Use of the Effective Schools Model for School Improvement," *Educational Leadership* 43, 1 (March 1985): 23-27.

Lezotte, Lawrence W. and Jo-Ann Cipriano Pepperl, *The Effective Schools Process: A Proven Path to Learning for All*. Effective Schools Products, Okemos, Michigan, 1999.

Maeroff, Gene, "Building Teams to Rebuild Schools," *Phi Delta Kappan* 74, 7 (March 1993): 512-519.

McCue, Lydia, *West Virginia Principals' Academy Notebook*. West Virginia Sate Department of Education, Charleston, West Virginia, 1987.

McNamara, James F., David A. Erlandson, and Maryanne McNamara, *Measurement & Evaluation: Strategies for School Improvement*. Eye on Education, New York, New York, 1999.

Morgan, Gareth, *Images of Organization*. Sage Publications, Beverly Hills, California, 1986.

Morgan, Gareth, *Imaginization: New Mindsets for Seeing, Organizing and Managing*. Sage Publications, San Francisco, California, 1997.

Morgan, Gareth, *Imaginization: The Art of Creative Management*. Sage Publications, Newbury Park, California, 1993.

Overview of the Common Body of Knowledge. Jackson (Mississippi) Public Schools Municipal Separate School District, 1985.

Peters, Thomas J. and Robert H. Waterman, Jr., *In Search of Excellence: Lessons from America's Best-Run Companies*. G.K. Hall & Co., Thorndike, Maine, 1997.

Ravitch, Diane, *Left Back: A Century of Failed School Reforms*. Simon & Schuster, New York, New York, 2000.

Ravitch, Diane and Joseph P. Viteritti, editors, *New Schools for a New Century: The Redesign of Urban Education*. Yale University Press, New Haven, Connecticut, 1997.

Ravitch, Diane and Joseph P. Viteritti, editors, *Making Good Citizens: Education and Civil Society*. Yale University Press, New Haven, Connecticut, 2001.

Reeves, Douglas B., *Accountability in Action: A Blueprint for Learning Organizations*. Advanced Learning Press, Denver, Colorado, 2000.

Renaissance Learning, Inc., Corporate Headquarters, PO Box 8036, Wisconsin Rapids, Wisconsin, 54495-8036 (http://www.renlearn.com).

Rheingold, Howard, *The Virtual Community: Homesteading on the Electronic Frontier*. The MIT Press, Cambridge, Massachusettes, 2000.

Ross, Richard B., "The Five Whys," *The Fifth Discipline Fieldbook* by Peter Senge, et al., Doubleday, New York, New York, 1994.

Rutter, Michael, Barbara Maughan, Peter Mortimore, and Janet Outston, *Fifteen Thousand Hours: Secondary Schools and Their Effects on Children*. Harvard University Press, Cambridge, Massachusetts, 1979.

Scearce, Carol, *100 Ways to Build Teams*. IRI/Skylight Publishing, Inc., Palentine, Illinois, 1992.

Schwab, Joseph J., "The Concept of the Structure of a Discipline," *Educational Record*, Vol. 43, July 1962.

Senge, Peter M., Art Kleiner, Charlotte Roberts, Richard B. Ross, and Bryan Smith, *The Fifth Discipline: The Art and Practice of the Learning Organization*. Doubleday, New York, New York, 1994.

Senge, Peter M., Nelda Cambron-McCabe, Timothy Lucas, Bryan Smith, Janis Dutton, and Art Kleiner, *Schools That Learn*. Doubleday, New York, New York, 2000.

Sergiovanni, Thomas, *Building Community in Schools*. Jossey-Bass Publishers, San Francisco, California, 1994.

Smith, Stuart C. and James J. Scott, *The Collaborative School: A Work Environment for Effective Instruction*. ERIC/CEM School Management Digest Series, No. 33, 1990.

Thornburg, David, *The New Basics: Education and the Future of Work in the Telematic Age*. Association for Supervision and Curriculum Development, Alexandria, Virginia, 2002.

Vogt, Judith F. and Kenneth L. Murrell, *Empowerment in Organizations: How to Spark Exceptional Performance*. University Associates, Inc., San Diego, California, 1990.

Wahlstrom, Deborah, *Using Data to Improve Student Achievement: A Handbook for Collecting, Organizing, Analyzing and Using Data*. Successline, Inc., Virginia Beach, Virginia, 1999.

Wang, Jia, "Opportunity to Learn: The Impacts and Policy Implications," *Educational Evaluation and Policy Analysis* 20, 3 (Fall 1998): 137-156.

Webb, Norman L. and Todd Bloom, "Report on Alignment," *Technical Report 98-1*. Center for the Study of Systemic Reform in Milwaukee Public Schools, Milwaukee, Wisconsin, 1998.

Weinstein, Rhona S., *Reaching Higher: the Power of Expectations in Schooling*. Harvard University Press, Cambridge, Massachusetts, 2002.

Wellins, Richard S., William C. Byham, and Jeanne M. Wilson, *Empowered Teams: Creating Self-Directed Work Groups That Improve Quality, Productivity, and Participation*. Jossey-Bass, Inc., San Francisco, California, 1991.

Woldman, Evelyn, technology coordinator for Massachusetts Elementary School Principals' Association, as interviewed by Mary Ann Zehr in "Screening for the Best," *Technology Counts '99*, a special publication by *Education Week* 19, 4: 13-22.